بسم الله الرحمن الرحيم

With the Heart in Mind

With the Heart in Mind

THE MORAL AND EMOTIONAL INTELLIGENCE OF THE PROPHET

MIKAEEL AHMED SMITH

Qalam

Printed in the United States of America
ISBN 978-1-7336256-0-9 (softcover)

Library of Congress Control Number: 2019932502

Published by
QALAM BOOKS
1148 W Pioneer Pkwy, Suite A
Arlington, TX 76013
www.qalambooks.com

Author	Mikaeel Ahmed Smith
Editing	Hashem Meriesh
Lead Designer	Amnah Sultan
Cover Concept	Fatimah Zahra Ahmed & Saffiyah Khan
Book Design	ARM (www.whitethreadpress.com)

DEDICATION

To all those whose hearts and eyes were blind
and then Allah blessed them with sight,
may this book sharpen your perception.

To all those who stumble in darkness
listening for any call to the path,
may this book introduce to you the guide.

To my teachers who grabbed my hand and pulled me
out of darkness and then taught me how to see again,
may this book please your hearts.

To my mother and my father
who continue to inspire me,
may you see in Muḥammad ﷺ
the divine gift of perfection in character.

Contents

Appreciation

I would never have been able to write this book had it not been for many special people who inspired me along the way. I am grateful to Allah for my lovely wife Sarah who continued to push me forward as I wrote the original manuscript. Had it not been for her encouragement and support, I am sure this book would not be here today. It would be a great injustice if I did not extend my gratitude to Dr. Nameera Akhtar who spent countless hours reviewing my research and challenging my ideas. I am deeply indebted to my primary research assistant Sister Rawa Awad for her meticulous research. It would be an understatement to say that her research forms the backbone of the emotional intelligence intersection with prophetic narrations. I would also like to thank Qalam Institute for supporting this project and providing me the opportunity to put this book together and lastly, a special thanks to my editors, Hashem Meriesh, Sally Elhousieny, and Asiya Ahmad. Thank you for your time, insight, and guidance.

Introduction

I begin this book by asking a simple question: "Who is the most intelligent person you know?" History is replete with men and women who we have tokenized as icons of intellect and reason, and for whom we sculpted prizes and awards to be placed within their hands as they are idolized before all, yet we have failed to answer the fundamental question, "What is intelligence and what is the role of the intellect?" It was Aristotle who felt that virtue could be found by understanding the correct function of a thing. An eye was deemed to be useful in so much as it could see. Likewise, the intellect will be deemed praiseworthy only in accordance with the fulfillment of its function. Therefore, we must define the role and function of the intellect before answering my initial question.

It is often the answers to life's simplest questions that are the most indicative of who we are, what we value, and how we understand the world around us. We are, therefore, obliged to question our assumptions, as they form the foundations of our worldview, even if only for the sole purpose of attempting to remain true to who we are or want to be.

My observation is that when this question is posed to even a religious Muslim, the answers that are given are people who are the furthest removed from religion. A 2013 study from the University of Rochester titled *The Relation Between Intelligence and Religiosity* found what they called a "negative association between intelligence and religiosity." This means that as people became more intelligent, they became less religious. The study offers three possible reasons for this finding:

1. More intelligent people are less likely to conform; thus they resist religious dogma,
2. They tend to be more analytical in their thinking which, as the study claims, has been shown to undermine religious belief,
3. And lastly, some of the key functions that religion serves in the lives of its adherents are conferred by intelligence, so intelligent people don't need religion.

This study took into consideration 63 other studies published between 1928 and 2012. Of these 63 studies, 53 reported that the more intelligent a person was, the more likely that person would shy away from religious belief. The ultimate conclusion made in this paper is perhaps the primary reason why I am writing this book. The authors conclude by saying,

> Most extant explanations (of a negative relation) share one central theme—the premise that religious beliefs are irrational, not anchored in science, not testable and, therefore, unappealing to intelligent people who "know better."

So why is the intellect assumed to be removed from theism? Beginning with John Locke and Baruch Spinoza, Western intellectuals attempted to divorce rationality from the soul. Locke and Spinoza led the way in declaring that thought was material and that the brain and the mind were one and the same. The psyche was no longer the soul; it became the mind. George Makari writes in *Soul Machine*, "Locke stripped the rational soul of its greatest attributes, forcefully repositioned the faculties of thought, memory, and consciousness into a rational faculty and thereby wished to distinguish passion ruled and superstition ruled fanatics from rational gentlemen." The study of *An Essay*

Concerning Human Understanding in 1689 attempted to completely alter how intellectuals understood the relationship between the body and the soul and, in the process, redefined intellect and intelligence. Borrowing the term from his teacher, Thomas Willis, Locke introduced the concept of thinking matter. By means of this, he was able to bring together two things that Descartes felt possessed "real distinction."

Regarding the relationship between body and soul, Cartesian philosophy falls in line with the division between the material body and the immaterial rational soul, as explained by Aristotle in *De Amina*. Descartes explained in *Meditations on First Philosophy* that his purpose in showing that the human mind or soul is distinct from the body was to refute those "irreligious people" who only have faith in mathematics and will not believe in the soul's immortality without a mathematical demonstration of it. The implications that Locke's division of body and soul would have for religion was clear for many. Makari writes that Locke received an "enraged letter" from Isaac Newton who had published his masterpiece six years prior. After reading Locke's essay, Newton was furious. According to him, Locke had destroyed morality and had "become an atheist." Later he apologized for his anger and continued to work against materialism.[1]

Locke's essay posed a clear threat to religion, imposing a boundary between science and religion. He himself remained devoted to Christianity, but it was this controversial essay which would later become the primary cause for materializing the immortal soul. Locke himself maintained the belief that humans possess an immaterial soul whose origin was divine. But with this essay, he stripped away perhaps the most defining aspect of the soul, its rationality, and named it the mind. Prior to Locke and Baruch Spinoza, the psyche was the soul, not the mind. The early philosophers who were followed by Descartes and others took a dualist approach to the soul and body. The Great Chain of Being or *scala naturæ* based on early philosophical thought

1 Makari, *Soul Machine*, p. 125.

placed all things in existence within a hierarchy based on the type of soul it possessed.

In *De Amina*, Aristotle divides all living beings into three types of souls: nutritive souls existing within plants, followed by sensitive souls existing within animals, and finally, the rational soul existing within human beings. This division can also be found within the Islamic tradition in the works of Rāzī, Ghazālī, Abū Zayd al-Balkhī, and Ibn Sīnā. Ibn Sīnā, who is best known for his commentary on Aristotle's *De Amina,* wrote a detailed explanation of the various types of souls called, *Kitāb al-Najāh*. Though many of the ideas he presents and explains are undoubtedly taken from his predecessors, Ibn Sīnā offers new explanations for some of the ideas and even develops the theory of prophethood upon some of Aristotle's ideas.

The soul is like a single genus, divisible in some ways into three parts. The first is the vegetative soul, which is the first entelechy (realization of potential). . .the second is the animal soul which is the entelechy of a natural body possessing organs in so much that it perceives individuals and moves by volition. . . the third is the human soul, which is the first entelechy of a natural body possessing organs in so far as it acts by rational choice and rational deduction and that it perceives universals.[2]

For Ibn Sīnā, the human being holds the highest position of the lower realm because he possesses a rational soul. Ibn Sīnā's breakdown of the various souls inspired some of the most well-known Qur'ānic exegesis.

If there is one verse of the Qur'ān that explicitly confers a position of supremacy to the children of Adam, it is the 70th verse of Sūrah Banī Isrā'īl.

> We have honored the children of Adam, and carried them on land and sea, and provided them with good things, and preferred them greatly over many of those who We created.

---

2 F. Rahman, *Avicenna's Psychology*, p. 09.

Commenting on this verse, the great exegete and scholar Fakhr al-Dīn al-Rāzī begins by explaining to his readers that human and animal life share five primary capacities: (1) needing nourishment, (2) growth, (3) reproduction, (4) sensory perception, and (5) the ability to move freely. Thereafter, he discusses what he sees as the foremost element that distinguishes humans from all other life:

> The human being is distinguished by another capacity. It is the rational or intellectual capacity which can reach the reality of things in existence as they actually are. It is within this capacity that the light of the gnosis of Allah is illuminated. It is within this capacity that the light of His greatness shines and it is this capacity which can look upon the secrets of the world of Allah's creation and His commands. This capacity is from that which was placed within us by the Purest and Holy.

Before we analyze this statement of Rāzī, let us look at the intellectual atmosphere and context within which he lived. Rāzī died in 1208 AD, about sixteen years prior to the birth of Thomas Aquinas and 500 years prior to the father of Moral Therapeutics, Phillippe Pinel. For Rāzī, the *ʿaql* was the foremost divine gift bestowed upon the children of Adam. His usage of the word *Jawhar* or substance to describe the *ʿaql* and his division of mind and soul seems to place him clearly among those who accepted a dualist approach to the mind and body. Similarly, the Cartesian and Ghazalian understanding was that the rational soul was immaterial and thus distinct from the material body.

On this issue, Descartes and Bacon fought a successful battle to change old patterns of thinking and overcome what they considered an intellectual blindness that stemmed from religious dogma. Bacon felt that the true basis of knowledge was the natural world and the information it provided the senses. Bacon shifted attention to the utility of knowledge and felt that knowledge consisted of power, not virtue. He felt virtue boiled down to the practical usefulness found in knowledge. It was Bacon who led the charge against the early philosophers for placing too much hope in the power of reason. Bacon's thoughts formed around the time of Descartes' philosophical revolution, which suggested that God's existence was known only secondarily to knowledge of the self. Descartes enthroned human reason as the highest of all authorities. Infallibility was shifted from revelation to reason. This global shift in thought was accurately and eloquently described by Richard Tarnas: "Here then, was the prototypical declaration of the modern self, established as a fully separate, self-defining entity, for whom its own rational self-awareness was absolutely primary—doubting everything except itself."[3]

It is also this worldview that considers certainty of any kind to be the lot of the unintelligent, and doubt or skepticism to be the ultimate goal of the intelligent. Certainty of any kind is considered an absurdity in this age, let alone certainty about that which is beyond the realm of the tangible. Realizing the limitations and errors of sensory perception, man sought refuge from doubt and error in the cave of his intellect and rational faculties to arrive at truth, but this too failed him. In our current age, the postmodern intellectual attempts to find peace while standing on the unstable lily pads of modern intellectualism.

The Qur'ānic story of Ibrāhīm contemplating the heavens, looking for his Creator, seems to foretell the plight of the modern man who wishes to arrive in the presence of the Divine through reason and empiricism. The beauty in Ibrāhīm's story involves his acknowledgment of the need for divine assistance to know more. Ibrāhīm realized the limits of his faculties and his intellect's dependence upon Allah. It is the role of revelation to reveal and illuminate that which is hidden from man. Just as physical sight is dependent on external light, so too does *ʿaql* need an external light for it to see.

The Islamic conception of prophethood challenges Descartes' enthroning of human reason as the ultimate authority and argues that true enlightenment results when the intellect is guided by revelation.

---

3 Tarnas, *The Passion of the Western Mind*, p. 280.

In contrast to Bacon's characterization that "knowledge is power," the Qur'ān highlights the primary function and benefit of the intellect as its ability to recognize Allah and submit to Him. In contrast to modernity and postmodernity, Islamic epistemology considers doubt to be a spiritual disease of the heart which, if left untreated, will torment the heart and soul of the one afflicted until death. Doubt is considered a darkness, like clouds blocking the light of the sun. This paradigm holds knowledge to be a divine light which illuminates the unknown, inside and outside the human being, with the ultimate source of that light being Allah. Allah addresses the modern obsession with doubt, stating from the beginning of the second chapter of the Qur'ān that "this is the Book in which there is no doubt."[4]

While I believe that Muslims are in dire need of understanding the forces that shape their worldviews, and the implications of those worldviews for their religious beliefs, that is not the primary purpose of this book. This book sets before readers a plausible construct for prophetic intelligence and, in particular, the intelligence of the Prophet Muḥammad ﷺ. The model for prophetic intelligence that we will put forward is one inspired through revelation. It was the *ʿaql* of the Prophet ﷺ, extraordinary in and of itself and perfected and harmonized by divine revelation, that caused massive changes in society during his lifetime, and it was this very same multifaceted, revelation-inspired intelligence that he strove to develop in his followers as well. Just as ripples are formed in water proportionate to the mass of an object dropped in it, so too has the coming of prophetic intelligence caused tidal waves of change in society, waves that flooded the hearts of those around the prophets of God, and also those that came many years after. Our focus on the intellect of the Prophet ﷺ and its importance by no means places the intellect above revelation. Just as the eye cannot see without external light so too is the intellect unable to understand without revelation.

4 Q 2: 2.

The *ʿaql* of the Prophet ﷺ illuminated the darkness within man, while also illuminating the darkness outside of him. If one can model and develop the multiple intelligences he possessed, one may also hope to become an agent of deep, radical change and influence.

We approach this topic by first separating the message from the messenger. Our claim is that the methods used by the Messenger to effect change deserve just as much attention as the message he was tasked to convey. This book is not only an investigation into the intellect of the Prophet ﷺ but an attempt to highlight why Islamic scholarship always considered him the most intelligent of Allah's creation. It is an attempt to reclaim the flag of intellectualism and place it within the hands of its rightful owners: the believers in God.

Throughout this book, we question competing understandings of intelligence and rationality and offer an alternative model that combines two distinct intelligences: moral and emotional. Prophetic intellect or *ʿaql* is the synthesis of these two intelligences into one reality. This construct of intellect revives the importance of reason and logic within the pedagogy of religious education. It also provides us with the missing link to behavioral changes within ourselves and others.

If you have never studied the life of the Prophet ﷺ, this book is an excellent place to start because it attempts to uncover the very core of his being, his message, and his understanding of those around him. For seasoned students of knowledge, it is hoped that they too will gain a deeper appreciation for the Prophet ﷺ after studying him from a perspective that is usually only presented marginally.

In Section 1, I present various Islamic and Western perspectives on the *ʿaql* and its role in human life. Qur'ānic appeals to the intellect are found over forty times throughout the text, forcing us to ask, "What is the purpose of the *ʿaql*?" Readers should walk away from Section 1 with a deeper appreciation for the emphasis placed on the development of the intellect in the Islamic scholastic tradition as well as a deeper understanding of what scholarship actually meant to the early generations. Most importantly, this section lays the framework for the two primary intelligences found within the prophetic model of intellect in an attempt to understand why people like Ghazālī went to the extent of claiming that prophethood was a completely intellectual affair. Wahb ibn Munabbih, while comparing the intelligence of the entire creation with the intelligence of the Prophet ﷺ said, "It is like one grain of sand compared to the sand of the entire earth." In this section, we also look at Howard Gardner's theory of multiple intelligences and how it relates to the Qur'ānic concept of *ʿaql*.

This brings us to Section II, the core of this book, in which we move our attention to the emotional intelligence of the Prophet ﷺ. It is this chapter that inspired my investigation into the *ʿaql* of the Prophet ﷺ. I wondered how he won the hearts of so many! Why did he say in a prophetic narration, "To love and be loved by people is half of intelligence?"[5] I realized that one's ability to cause change and influence others is based solely on this intelligence. I was further encouraged to write this particular section after witnessing a problem within myself. I noticed that I lacked the ability to deeply connect with the people around me. I lacked the ability to understand the ones who I claimed to love the most. I wondered why I struggled with this problem. The shallowness of my relationships was even more troublesome because I claimed to follow a Prophet who, based on my research and based on the testimony of thousands of eyewitnesses, was a master of deep connection and understanding. How could I follow in his footsteps and inspire change in the hearts of others without fixing this problem? So, I began studying the life of the Prophet ﷺ solely from the perspective of emotional intelligence. It is the absence of this particular side of the *ʿaql* that has deeply strained the bonds connecting our families and communities and stripped us of our ability to effectively convey the message of Islam cross-culturally. This type of intelligence is absolutely necessary for American Muslim communities due to their extreme diversity. Navigating the cultural fault lines within our communities requires a deep emotional intelligence.

---

5 Bayhaqī, *Shuʿab al-Īmān*, vol. 6, p. 376.

Section III covers the cornerstone of the ʿ*aql*: moral intelligence. This is the aspect of the ʿ*aql* that lays down the framework for recognizing and adopting ethical truths and provides a person with the ability to hold true to those ideals. I consider moral intelligence to be the cornerstone of the ʿ*aql* because, without it, emotional intelligence is simply a tool for selfish influence and manipulation. Moral intelligence is complex, as it involves establishing a criterion within people by which they recognize truth and falsehood and building within them the ability to remain committed to those ideals and to solve problems based on that established criterion. Undoubtedly, subjective morality has deeply damaged the collective ethos of our society. Islam's bold declaration of right and wrong is increasingly viewed as intrusive or suffocating, and the lack of communal conformity regarding the appropriateness and inappropriateness of behaviors has resulted in an unstable and confused society. For all intents and purposes, the words "should" and "ought" have been taken out of the dictionary completely because there is no external standard of appropriateness other than one's own self. Simply put, many believe and say, "I should only do what I feel is appropriate."

In the final section, we will be discussing single- and double-loop learning and how these two levels of learning relate to the emotional components of emotional intelligence. How did the Prophet ﷺ affect his society and cause such dramatic change in such a short period of time? How did he cause such *radical change*? It is my hope that this last section will be of greatest benefit to teachers and parents. These two groups of people, in my estimation, stand in the best position to cause social and individual reform. Fortunately, by studying and implementing the methods used by the Prophet ﷺ, one can be sure that the changes they inspire will be meaningful.

Standing before hundreds of thousands of his companions on the mountain of ʿArafah during his Farewell Sermon, the Prophet ﷺ sought confirmation from his people that he had indeed fulfilled the trust given to him. From the top of the mountain, he asked, "Have I conveyed the message?" They replied, "Indeed you have!" Then, with his finger pointed to the heavens, he said, "O Allah, bear witness! O Allah, bear witness! O Allah, bear witness!" Because his companions witnessed his methods and were radically changed by them, they were able to use those same methods to pass the message to others. My main objective in this book is to make you bear witness as well.

THE MOST INTELLIGENT

It's the summer of 2006 and I'm walking through the streets of Rukn al-Dīn, a small area in Damascus surrounding the Abū Nūr University. Rukn al-Dīn, or Pillar of Faith, was a small neighborhood within the city of Damascus. Amidst the hustle and bustle of students of sacred knowledge coming and going to class, carrying books and notebooks, I felt as if I had officially become part of this sacred tradition of learning. As I walked through the alleys of Rukn al-Dīn, it seemed as if every other shop I passed by was a bookstore. I had just arrived a week earlier, and by now, I was comfortable in this distinct yet beautiful new world and began to interact more and more with anyone I could. I came to Damascus to improve my Arabic and to spend time with Shaykh Rajab Deeb, a well-known and respected scholar of the city. Trying to fully experience the Damascene student life, I walked into one of the many bookstores. "*Al-Salām ʿalaykum*," I said as I walked into the tiny bookstore crammed with books. The young clerk replied without glancing my way and I began to rummage through the books. I was just beginning to learn Arabic at the time, and having spent about two years studying in a traditional *madrasah*, I could barely read the titles of the books. In hindsight, I realize that my American gait and body language must have been far more pronounced than I understood.

"Can I help you?" the young clerk asked as I put down a book.

"Um, yes. I'm looking for a book called *al-Shifā*," I said in the most broken Arabic imaginable.

I had not come to the bookstore with the intent of buying *al-Shifā*, but it was the first title that came to mind. "Of course!" the young man replied as he pulled a thick book from the shelf and handed it to me. I was amazed at the beauty of the thick book, the Arabic words written in gold letters surrounded by soft blue.

As I was just beginning to learn Arabic at the time, it was well beyond my level of comprehension. I purchased the book simply because I had once heard it referenced during a lecture. I found the particular quote so intriguing that the name of the book was etched into my memory. *al-Shifā*, a well-known book about the Prophet ﷺ, was written by the Andalusian scholar, Qāḍī ʿIyāḍ. I bought that book along with others, and when I reached my apartment I began to look for the quote that had been engraved in my mind ever since I had first heard it. I had no idea where in the book I would find this statement, but I knew one word from the quote: *ʿaql*. It took very little time before I came across the section discussing the unique and superior intellect of the Prophet Muḥammad ﷺ. It was in this section that I found the quote:

> Wahb ibn Munabbih said, "I have studied over seventy different books. After reading all of them, I have come to the conclusion that from the first man to the last, the intelligence which was given to all of humanity when compared to the intelligence of the Prophet Muḥammad ﷺ is like that of a grain of sand compared to the sand of the entire world. He was, indeed the most intelligent man."

This statement told me that the more I learned and read, the more I would come to the realization that he, Muḥammad ﷺ, was the most intelligent of Allah's creation.

It wasn't until fourteen years later that I began studying theories of multiple intelligences, theories that claimed that intelligence was actually a collection of multiple capacities such as social intelligence, moral intelligence, and emotional intelligence. Having studied the life of Prophet Muḥammad ﷺ, I began to understand that the Islamic understanding of an ideal, complete intelligence was one that facilitated recognition of Allah, promoted moral reform, and provided its owner with the ability to understand other people.

Over the last ten years, the utility and importance of emotional, social, and moral intelligence have become widely appreciated. Numerous popular magazines and academics praise emotional quotient (EQ, as distinct from IQ, intelligence quotient) as the most sought-after quality employers are seeking these days. Our technological advancements in communication have made it easier to communicate, yet the impersonal and detached aspect of many of these modes of communication have negatively affected our ability to understand one another. With more time spent behind computer screens and less time communicating face-to-face, employers are now forced to train people on how to properly interact with others.

The more I studied these three intelligences, the more I began to realize that they were perfected in the character and teachings of the Prophet Muḥammad ﷺ. Narration after narration seemed to reiterate the depth of the Prophet's ﷺ intelligence. It seemed as if I was being asked to reflect deeper on the statement I had read a decade before about the Prophet's ﷺ intelligence being greater than that of the rest of creation. Was this statement referring to his ability to master his own emotions? His awareness of the emotions of others? His mastery of the other various aspects of intelligence? Could Wahb ibn Munabbih's understanding of *ʿaql* be congruent with the idea of multiple intelligences, or perhaps even more complex and profound than Gardner's theory, a theory that would not be completely developed until the 20th century?

I
ʿAql

As I approached the closed door, the silence of the classroom gave me the impression that my teacher might have already begun the lesson. "You did it again," I thought to myself. "Every time you sleep after *fajr*, you wake up late for class," I whispered to myself, not knowing if the teacher had arrived before me or not. Normally, a silent classroom was a clear sign that the teacher had arrived and had begun his lesson. It was amazing how fast we would quiet down the moment our teachers walked in the classroom. This was likely rooted in the Qur'ānic verse, "Do not raise your voices above the voice of the Prophet," and for us, our teachers were the closest we could get to the Prophet ﷺ; they were our link to him. Whatever the reason, the class was pin-drop silent as I approached the door. I opened it, and sure enough, all of my classmates were sitting around the Shaykh, with their legs folded beneath them and their books open in front of them.

Students of prophetic traditions or *Hadīth* observe an amazingly high level of respect while they read the traditions before their teachers. Normally the students will read before the teacher as the teacher quietly listens closely to the correct enunciation of the Arabic text. Occasionally the teacher will stop the reader and explain various aspects of the tradition. Sometimes, however, an entire class could go by without the teacher sharing any deeper insights. Slowly closing the door behind me, I kept my gaze to the floor, hoping my tardiness would be excused and overlooked as I found my place and sat down. I quietly opened my book, trying not to bring the slightest attention to my presence. Our desks were very low to the ground, just high enough for our folded legs to fit under them. I breathed a sigh of relief as my classmate continued to read. I knew that if the teacher allowed me to sit down, this was a sign of him excusing my tardiness. For us, mere permission to sit in class was the highest honor. Just as I began to relax, my teacher stopped teaching and, mid-sentence, he looked up at me. "It seems like you didn't do *wuḍū'* before you came," he said with a slight tone of amazement. "How did I forget to make *wuḍū'*?" I thought to myself. I was so concerned about getting to class on time that I had forgotten. I remained silent, of course. "Knowledge is light from one heart to the next. You will never gain knowledge without spiritual purification. Go make *wuḍū'*," he said in a soft manner, slightly smiling.

> The scholars say, "*ʿAql* is a light which Allah created as a faculty and quality. It is with the *ʿaql* that you see and by it that you articulate." They also say, "The *ʿaql* is a light in the heart just as sight is a light in the eyes."

This vivid memory from my days as a student sheds some light on the normative Islamic understanding of one aspect of the intellect: intelligence involves knowledge of the Divine. The Islamic tradition considers intellect to be the medium by which one knows Allah and knows His commands. The intellect guides one to His Presence.

It is impossible to present the entirety of the Islamic perspective on the *ʿaql* within this one book. My aim is much humbler than that. It is simply to expose the reader to the rich complexity in the discussions that took place regarding the *ʿaql* in early Islamic literature and to present a model of prophetic intelligence that combines moral sight and strength with emotional intelligence and understanding.

The seventh section of the first chapter of Abū Ḥamid al-Ghazālī's masterpiece *Revival of the Islamic Sciences* is titled *The Intellect: Its Nobility and Reality and Aspects.* In this section, Ghazālī paints a lucid picture of the Islamic understanding of the intellect. He says,

> Know that this is among the things which do not require one to take pains in bringing to light. . .Intellect is the spring and starting point of knowledge. The intellect is the seat of knowledge, and it is by means of knowledge we are guided.[6]

Ghazālī felt that the nobility of the intellect could be witnessed by looking at what resulted from the intellect (i.e., knowledge and understanding.) I was unaware at the time, but when my teacher compared knowledge to light, he was simply passing on the very basic yet essential understanding that the function of knowledge is to illuminate. After stating that the nobility of the intellect is self-evident, Ghazālī turns his attention to revelation,

> However, our purpose is to relate what has been conveyed by the Hadith of the Prophet ﷺ, and the verses of the Qur'ān concerning its virtue. Allah called it (intellect) "light" in the verse, "Allah is the light of the heavens and the earth, a semblance of His light is a niche. . ." and the knowledge that is acquired from the intellect is called a spirit, revelation, and a life. Allah says in the Qur'ān,[7] "Is he who was dead and We raised him to life, and set for him a light by which he walks among men, the same as one in darkness from which he will not come out?"[8]

This illuminating characterization of knowledge and its practical implications for human ethics will be discussed in detail as we analyze both Ghazālī's and Muḥāsibī's theories of the intellect.

---

6 Ghazālī, *Iḥyā' ʿUlūm al-Dīn*, Vol. 1, p. 305.

7 Ghazālī, *Iḥyā' ʿUlūm al-Dīn*, vol. 1, p. 305.

8 Q 6:122.

MUḤĀSIBĪ'S THEORY OF INTELLIGENCE

A large crowd has slowly formed, gathering around a young scholar as he and his father passionately argue in the street of the heavily populated *Bāb al-Ṭāq* district located in the upper east side of Baghdad. *Bāb al-Ṭāq* was the young scholar's neighborhood, and while he was well known throughout the city of Baghdad, he was particularly popular here. This neighborhood was one of prestige and wealth and was located on the eastern bank of the Tigris River. It had not always been such a distinguished area of the city; it was only after Caliph Manṣūr moved his caliphal residence out of the immaculate Round City did the east side of Baghdad become so prominent.

After Manṣūr's death, the next caliph, Mahdi, lived in the new caliphal residence and also moved the remaining official administrative offices east of the Tigris, slightly north of the caliphal residence in an area known as Rusāfah. *Bāb al-Ṭāq,* the district where the current argument is taking place, was beautifully located just south of Rusāfah and north of the caliphal residence, making it a place of prime real estate. The area became so populated that Mahdi was forced to decree that a large commercial district be built to support the extensive growth.

This argument is now taking place during the reign of Hārūn al-Rashīd and his Chief Justice, Abū Yūsuf, the leading student of Abū Ḥanīfa, who happens to be the teacher of the young man arguing with his father.[9]

"Father, you must, you have no choice."

"Son, please listen to me; there is no need for such drastic measures," responds his father.

"Divorce my mother, Father, you must!" the young man exclaims to his father as onlookers gather to watch the drama unfold.

"I will do no such thing, son."

---

9 Dhahabī, *Siyar A'lām al-Nubalā',* vol. 9, p. 488.

"Father, by Allah, you are following a different religion than she is; your marriage is void."

While such a heated discussion in the open streets of the wealthiest district at the heart of the Muslim empire may seem unusual, this was unfortunately in line with the theological climate of that time, and it would only get worse over the reign of the next series of caliphs. By the time Muʿtaṣim became caliph in 218 AH/833 CE, the theological-scholastic debates of Hārūn's time, which were dividing families, had become theocratic policies and resulted in the imprisonment of scholars and state-sponsored torture.

The young scholar arguing in the street with his father was Muḥāsibī—a scholar and luminary who would eventually become a well-regarded source of knowledge in a number of Islamic sciences. Our discussion regarding the early Islamic understanding of the intellect begins with his theory of intelligence. His geographical location, the time in which he lived, and the general acceptance of his literary works within the ranks of Islamic scholarship make him an ideal source for studying the early Islamic understanding of the intellect.

At the time of this very public disagreement, Muḥāsibī's name was already well known throughout Baghdad. After studying the outer sciences, he turned his attention completely toward the inner dimensions of the heart and spiritual uprightness. His lectures were powerful, shaking the depths of listeners' hearts and causing tears to flow uncontrollably. Ismāʿīl ibn Isḥāq, also a scholar in the neighborhood, would periodically invite Muḥāsibī to his house for gatherings of reflection and remembrance of Allah. Aḥmad ibn Ḥanbal, a friend of Ismāʿīl's who had heard of Muḥāsibī's reputation and deep insight, desired a closer look.

"I hear Muḥāsibī comes to your house occasionally?" inquired Aḥmad ibn Ḥanbal.

"Yes, he does," replied Ismāʿīl to the esteemed Imam.

"Do you think it would be possible for me to attend the next gathering inconspicuously so that Muḥāsibī is unaware of my presence?"

"Of course," replied Ismāʿīl, delighted that his house would be blessed with the presence of two of the greatest scholars of his time.

Ismāʿīl said, "I immediately went to Muḥāsibī and asked him if it was possible for him and his students to have a gathering at my house that evening to which he agreed. They came between the *maghrib* prayer and the *ʿishā'* prayer, but Aḥmad ibn Ḥanbal had already arrived well before them. I seated him in a room which allowed him to see and hear everything that took place unbeknownst to those in attendance. After they prayed the evening prayer, they all sat quietly before Muḥāsibī in a state of deep meditation, with their heads hung down between their shoulders. This continued for almost half the night. Then one of the attendees asked a question, and Muḥāsibī began to speak about asceticism and piety. Those in attendance began to cry and moan as his words penetrated their hearts. I decided to go check on Aḥmad ibn Ḥanbal, who I found also weeping so profusely that he was close to fainting. After the morning prayer, they left, and I went to Aḥmad ibn Ḥanbal. 'So what do you think of him, Abū ʿAbd Allāh?' I asked him. 'I have never heard someone speak of piety and righteousness as this man, and I have not witnessed such people as those with him. That being said, I still feel that you should avoid their company.'"

In order to understand Aḥmad ibn Ḥanbal's disapproval of Muḥāsibī, we have to understand the religious climate of their city and time. Aḥmad ibn Ḥanbal and Muḥāsibī both witnessed the rise of the Rationalist (*Muʿtazili)* movement, but their reactions to it were quite different. Let us look back to the time of Manṣūr who, while laying the first brick of his Round City, also set the scene for centuries of strife.

THE FOUNDATIONS OF THEOLOGICAL STRIFE

In 145 AH/762 CE about twenty years before the birth of both Aḥmad ibn Ḥanbal and Muḥāsibī, Manṣūr became the caliph of the Muslim empire. The son of a *Tābiʿī*,[10] Abū Jaʿfar al-Manṣūr was a man of religious learning, having studied under his father and other scholars of Ḥadith of his time. Suyūtī said about him in *Tārīkh al-Khulafā'* that "he was very intelligent and a scholar of *fiqh* and literature."[11] Imam Mālik said, regarding the religious knowledge of Manṣūr,

> One day, Manṣūr and I became engaged in a conversation regarding the early scholars and the righteous people of the early generations, and I found him to be extremely knowledgeable. We began to discuss *fiqh,* and he had a very broad understanding of both the agreed-upon issues and the issues upon which there was a difference of opinion.[12]

He was especially fond of the science of Hadith, so much so that he sent his brother Mahdi, who would later become the caliph himself, to Madīna to study the *Muwatta'* under Imam Mālik. Historical reports tell us that, while performing the pilgrimage, Manṣūr met with Imam Mālik and begged him to write a Hadith book. Soon after this incident, the *Muwatta'* was prepared. According to Dhahabī, in 143 AH/760 CE, just two years before Manṣūr would become the caliph, the codification of *fiqh* and *tafsīr* began. Other sciences were also being codified at this time. Abū Ḥanīfa, already a resident of Baghdad, refused to take the position of Chief Justice of the empire when requested by Manṣūr, and wrote his book, *al-Fiqh al-Akbar,* around this time as well.

Although Manṣūr was known for being much more frugal than his Abbasid predecessors, he surpassed almost all of them in his love for knowledge and learning. While he closed the treasury to what he

---

10 A person who met a companion of Prophet Muḥammad ﷺ

11 Suyūtī, *Tārīkh al-Khulafā'*, p. 198.

12 Qutayba, *al-Imāma wa al-Siyāsa* (Vol. 2).

felt was unnecessary spending, he left no stone unturned to aid in educational advancement. This included having the most important books of knowledge that were not available in Arabic translated and sent to him. At this time, Baghdad did not have the resources necessary to have the works translated. Caesar commissioned the project, and books of philosophy written in various languages were translated. Persian, Greek, and Syriac books were all translated and sent to the caliph. The books were passed on to the scholars of the time working under the caliph who worked to develop the *ʿaqli* sciences for both the general population and the educated class.

Thousands of scholars migrated to this city of knowledge and learning in order to be part of the educational projects that were taking place, and Manṣūr continued to open the treasury for all educational projects, beginning the greatest intellectual expansion the Muslim world had ever seen. Of course, he had no idea what the consequences of this intellectual expansion would be, and the turmoil that he would inadvertently cause. Not only were books on Philosophy translated but books regarding Greek medicine, ethics, and mathematics were translated as well. In 154 AH/771 CE, a leading mathematician of India was summoned to the royal court to bring a Sanskrit work of *zij,* or mathematical tablet. From this, Muḥammad ibn Ibrāhīm al-Fazārī was commissioned to write what later became known as *Zīj al-Sindhind al-Kabīr* or the "Great Astronomical Tables of the Sindhind."

Manṣūr's time as caliph was short-lived. In 158 AH/775 CE, he passed away on his way to perform the pilgrimage, but his spirit of commitment to the rational sciences would survive him. His brother Mahdi followed in his elder brother's footsteps, continuing the enormous expansion in knowledge and intellectual activity in the Muslim world.

Muḥāsibī was born sometime around 165 AH/782 CE in the city of Basrah and passed away in the city of Baghdad in 243 AH/857 CE. He is considered one of the early imams of theology and *taṣawwuf.* Prior to diving into the ocean of spiritual knowledge, Muḥāsibī studied Islamic jurisprudence under some of the most well-known figures in Islamic scholarship. As a direct student of Imam Shāfiʿī and Abū Yūsuf, he was universally acknowledged as being a highly-skilled jurist. Tamīmī[13] said regarding his juristic knowledge, "He is an imam of the believers in juristic issues as well as spirituality and theology."[14] Nonetheless, he was very critical of the jurists at the same time, believing their knowledge of the permissible and impermissible blinded and deluded them and blocked them from seeing value in other types of important knowledge. He was the teacher of Junayd and a scholar of *kalām* and Hadith. Ibn Ḥajr writes about him that, "Ḥārith al-Muḥāsibī was an imam of Hadith and *kalām*." However, he became best known for his spiritual knowledge and asceticism. His books on the inner dimensions of Islamic spirituality ultimately became the inspiration for some of the most well-known texts on spirituality ever written. He was an exceptional orator. People who sat in his gatherings would say that it was as if he could make them see and feel whatever it was that he was talking about. This ability can also be found in his literary works as well. One of his books, *Tawahhum* (Imagination), is a first-person account of all that will take place after death based on the statements of the Qur'ān and prophetic narrations, as well as the author's imagination. Reading this book, one immediately senses what a gifted communicator he was.

Muḥāsibī would have only been about five years old when Hārūn al-Rashīd became the caliph in 170 AH/787 CE, but it had been over 20 years since the first books of metaphysics, such as Aristotle's *De Amina*, were passed around the tables of educated Muslims. By now, a generation of Muslim children had grown accustomed to and familiar with the names of ancient Hindu mathematicians and Greek philosophers, along with their philosophical dilemmas. Then, during the early reign of Hārūn, something unprecedented happened: the first paper mill began to produce paper in this city of knowledge and learning. This helped accelerate the spread of the Rationalist ideology. It was the

13 Abū Manṣūr ʿAbd al-Qāhir al-Tamīmī al-Baghdādī.

14 Ibid.

wealthy, educated classes who were the first to adopt the new creed of the Rationalists. This class would soon hold key positions close to the caliphs, leading to the adoption of the Rationalist ideology by the state. As a young man, Muḥāsibī frequented the gatherings of the Hadith scholars and traditionalists such as Abū Yūsuf and others, which was one of the primary factors for his deep animosity toward the Rationalists. His father, on the other hand, adopted some of the Rationalists' ideas while his mother stayed committed to the traditional understanding of theology. It was in this context that the heated argument took place on the streets of *Bāb al-Ṭāq* as Muḥāsibī pleaded with his father to either come back to traditional Islam or divorce his mother.

The Rationalists had destroyed the home of Muḥāsibī. When his father died, Muḥāsibī refused to accept his inheritance even though he was in dire need of the money. He quoted the Prophet ﷺ, who said, "People of different religions do not inherit from one another."[15] Convinced of the errors in the Rationalist ideology, Muḥāsibī devoted himself to publicly exposing them and mastered the field of *kalām* (theology) in the process. *Kalām*, as a science, was considered a risky field because of the discussions that it opened up and because it spoke about creedal issues in a manner that had not been previously entertained. Imam Aḥmad's apparent disapproval of the great Muḥāsibī was primarily due to his heavy involvement in this science. But seeing what the Rationalist movement had done to the family of Muḥāsibī, one can understand why he was so passionate about refuting their tenets.

Beginning our discussion of the *ʿaql* with Muḥāsibī is ideal for two reasons. Firstly, by studying someone from the first generation of Islamic scholarship, we are catching a glimpse of a primary source understanding of the intellect—a primary source who fought to reclaim the flag of intellectualism from the Rationalist school of thought. Reading Muḥāsibī's works provides a glimpse at what would

15 Tirmidhī, *Sunan al-Tirmidhī*, vol. 3, p. 496.

have been popular literature in Baghdad and the rest of the Muslim empire. Secondly, Muḥāsibī lived during the rising influence of the Rationalists and was therefore very familiar with them and their twisted ideologies which destroyed his own home. In 232 AH/847 CE, he was forced to leave Baghdad and move to Kūfa due to a major political power shift in favor of the Rationalists. This did not stop Muḥāsibī from criticizing and challenging the Rationalists' positions. Central to the Rationalists' understanding was the primacy of the *ʿaql* and the idea that the *ʿaql* had a more authoritative position than divine revelation.

If we take a look at Muḥāsibī's *Theory of Intelligence,* we see a very complex and multifaceted understanding of the intellect, which clearly reflects the time within which he lived. During Muḥāsibī's era, there were multiple competing views regarding the intellect. Muḥāsibī lived during the same time as Wāṣil, the founder of the Rationalist School, but he also lived around the *Mutakallimūn* or scholars of *kalām* who debated against the Rationalists in the arena of theology. The *Mutakalimūn* inclined toward a position on the intellect that was prevalent among the *ṣufis*, who considered the *ʿaql* as a means of recognizing the benefits of obeying Allah's commandments. The Rationalists, on the other hand, took a purely rational, Hellenistic approach, stating that the *ʿaql mujarrad*, the unaided intellect, was sufficient for distinguishing good from evil. In detail, the *Sufi* perspective, to which Muḥāsibī leaned, viewed the intellect as a quality placed within the human being by Allah, which, from one perspective, was independently capable of deciphering basic good and evil. This view was later adopted by the Māturīdī theological school, which we will discuss in the coming sections. They also opined that the intellect was something that was able to recognize the benefits of obeying commands of Allah and the benefits of avoiding that which was prohibited by Allah. This is clear from the writings of Muḥāsibī and others who were very close to him. Aḥmad ibn ʿĀṣim al-Anṭākī, a close friend of Muḥāsibī, wrote regarding the *ʿaql*, "The most beneficial intelligence is that which recognizes the blessings of Allah and helps you show gratitude towards Him, and which stands opposed to your desires." When asked about the *ʿaql*, Sarī al-Saqaṭī, the master of Junayd, similarly replied, "It is that reality by which the proof of the command and prohibition is established." Another close friend of Muḥāsibī, Ibn Masrūq, wrote, "Whoever does not use his intellect to protect himself from his intellect will be destroyed by his intellect." This final quote summarizes quite well how Muḥāsibī and others during his time viewed the intellect and rejected the Rationalist approach.

MUḤĀSIBĪ'S THEORY OF INTELLIGENCE

Muḥāsibī's *Theory of Intelligence* is primarily based on the description of the *ʿaql* found within the Qur'ān, Sunnah and early works of exegesis. Together, these sources provided Muḥāsibī and his contemporaries with a construct of the intellect that was completely different from that of the Rationalist school. Throughout the Qur'ān, there are various nominal forms used for the intellect, and these words are found thirty-four times in the text. While the noun *ʿaql* is not found in the Qur'ān, its verbal form occurs forty-six times. The majority of those mentions are connected to contemplation of the signs of Allah, such as the natural world, planetary movements and celestial bodies, and the remnants of past nations. In these verses, Allah calls upon the *ʿaql* to reflect upon these things and deduce from them reflections of the greatness of Allah. Even everyday phenomena, such as the alternation between day and night, are objects of reflection and contemplation for the *ʿaql*. In some of these verses, it is the actions and habitual states that we experience that we are called to contemplate, such as sleeping at night and working and playing throughout the day. In other verses, it is the actions of animals that are the focus. Allah tells us that these aspects of the world are signs for the intellect to reflect upon. Once a person has logically arrived at acknowledgment of the Creator, then rationality demands that one's actions be consistent with that knowledge. Individual and societal behavior, along with upright actions, should be based on a cognitive certainty of the Creator's presence. For this reason, we find that Allah calls into question the intellectual capacities of those who have not obtained knowledge of Allah through His signs and the intellectual capacities of those who know but do not act in accordance with that knowledge. In summary, rationality demands consistency.

Muḥāsibī understood *ʿaql* as referring to three different levels:

1. The first level of intellect, that which is given directly by Allah to those considered responsible for their actions,
2. the second level is *fahm* or understanding,
3. the third level involves *baṣirah* or insight.

The First level

Muḥāsibī's first point is that the *ʿaql* is a *garīza*; that is, an innate quality found within all human beings. In his book *Māhiyya al-ʿaql*, Muḥāsibī explains that this position is different than the position of some of the *mutakallimūn* of his time, who said that the intellect was the actual soul of the human being. His position also refuted another view of his time that the intellect was *maʿrifah*, recognition itself. Refuting this claim, he said, "According to us, it (the intellect) is an innate quality, and recognition is a product of this quality. . . the intellect is an innate quality while recognition is an action."[16] Nevertheless, Muḥāsibī does attest to the intrinsic connection between the intellect and recognition. By stating that recognition is a "necessary function of the intellect," he is simply highlighting the distinction between a cause and its effect. He deduces this from the Qur'ānic passages in which Allah asks the Angels to tell him the names of the things He had created.

> [Recall the time] When your Lord told the angels: "I am setting on the earth a vicegerent." They asked: "Will you put there one that

16 Muḥāsibī is simply pointing out that the intellect cannot logically be an action.

> will work evil and shed blood; when we praise You and sanctify Your name?" He replied: "Surely I know what you know not." He taught Adam the names {of all things, and their usefulness], and then showed them to the angels: "Tell me the names of these if you are truthful." "Transcendent are You!" they replied. "We have no knowledge except that which You have given us. You alone are the Knowing, the Wise."[17]

The Angels had not been taught the names, so they admitted their inability and ignorance. On the other hand, when Adam was given the same task, he was able to name the things before him. "He recognized by means of his intellect and was thereby able to differentiate between meanings."[18] The untrained intellect would be unable to differentiate between the things it sees; i.e., it could not recognize anything. Conceptualization is the central ability of the intellect. In order for a person to be able to learn, one must be able to think of things abstractly. If I say the word "man," any person who speaks English should be able to form a mental image of a male human being. Conceptualization gives one the ability to categorize all new information. Immediately, one is able to look at any adult male human and state, "This is a man." Adam did not have to be taught the names of everything that would ever come into existence because, through the gift of the *ʿaql* and learning, he would be able to recognize everything. But an intellect deprived of the ability to learn would, like the Angels, be forced to say, "I have no knowledge." Islamic philosophical thought was profoundly impacted by this position as many great intellectuals such as Aḥmad ibn Ḥanbal, Ibn Taymiyya,[19] and Jamāl al-Dīn al-Jawzī[20] ended up following this view of Muḥāsibī.[21]

But how do we know we have an *ʿaql* in the first place? Muḥāsibī

17 Q 2:30–32.

18 Muḥāsibī, *Māhiyyat al-ʿAql*, p. 206.

19 Ibn Taymīya, *al-Radd ʿalā al-Manṭiqiyyīn*, p. 94.

20 Jamāl al-Dīn al-Jawzī, *Kitāb al-Adhkiyāʾ*, p. 10.

21 Muḥāsibī, *Māhiyyat al-ʿAql*, p. 204.

would explain that there is no way to "know about the presence of the *ʿaql* (within a person) except by means of the *ʿaql*," meaning that it is only by means of thinking and contemplation that we know we have an intellect. Muḥāsibī claims that we have no tool of recognition other than the intellect, which means that the intellect itself recognizes its own existence. His justification for this view is as follows:

> The reason for this is that if the recognition of external things, which are perceived by the senses, is dependent upon the *ʿaql*, then the recognition *of* the *ʿaql* cannot be dependent upon anything other than itself.[22]

We will speak in much more detail about this point when we look at Ghaẓālī's understanding of the *ʿaql* in upcoming sections. Another term Muḥāsibī used to explain this first meaning was *nūr* or light. He actually combined two terms together when explaining the *ʿaql* and said that it is *nūr garīzah*—an implanted light—within the creation by which we see and express that which we know. He felt that just as the eyes had sight, a natural quality placed within the majority of the creation, the intellect, too, was a natural quality placed within the majority of the creation by which to see. This innate aspect of the intellect is critical to Islamic theology because accountability before Allah is dependent upon this basic level which differentiates children from adults and a sound intellectual capacity from an unsound one. He takes this to such an extent that he says, "It is the intellect which is the sole addressee of the revelation."

Muḥāsibī felt that three actions were the exclusive functions of the *ʿaql*: speech, deduction, and choice. He argues that speech is an act of the intellect because the construction of intelligible sentences and the formation of arguments demands logical thought and reason. Perhaps this is why the word for logic in both Arabic (*manṭiq*) and Greek

22 The Imam is referring to our metacognitive capacity. Our ability to think about our thinking is an exclusively human phenomenon and we know we have an intellect because we have this unique ability to make our thoughts the subject matter of our thoughts.

(*legein*) are derived from the root "to speak." If speech is exclusively a function of the intellect, it would explain the Islamic pedagogical emphasis on extensive education in grammar and rhetoric.

The second action of the intellect is deduction, the ability to extract meanings from the information it gains through its senses. Muḥāsibī explains that it is by the action of deduction that the *ʿaql* is aware of its own existence. The same concept was explained many centuries later when Descartes famously said, "I think, therefore I am." The ability to separate and categorize things is an ability that is only possible if a person has an intellect that can deduce meanings. In Urdu, a word used for behavior is *tamyīz*, which comes from the Arabic root *ma-ya-za* which means to separate one thing from another. A child or an adult who doesn't know how to act in a given situation is called *bad-tamyīz*, which means one lacking the capacity to distinguish appropriate conduct from inappropriate conduct. Similarly, in Arabic, we find the term *sinn al-tamyīz,* which means the age of discrimination. Looking across cultures and generations, we see that human beings, for the most part, absolve children of legal responsibility. The reason is that they have not developed the ability to completely deduce which actions are appropriate in which settings. They lack a mature *ʿaql* that has developed the ability to distinguish.

The last action of the intellect is choice. As the *ʿaql* learns about the world and performs the first two actions of speaking and deducing, the human being is then forced to choose. Even the choice not to do anything is based on speech and deduction. These three functions of the *ʿaql* are the essence of educational systems where we begin by learning the names of things, places, and feelings. We ask our parents and teachers, "What is this and what is that?", building vocabulary and basic understanding of ourselves and the world around us and developing our reading, writing, and speaking skills so that we can learn more about the world. Thereafter we ask "Why?" "Why" is the resultant question of the second action of the *ʿaql*. I remember the first time my daughter saw someone smoking and asked what they were doing. I said, "Smoking." "What does it do to you?" she replied. I explained that the person smoking might say that it makes them feel good. "What else does it do?" she asked. "It hurts your body and can give you cancer," I explained. Through these questions, the "what" was answered, and the first action of the *ʿaql* was completed. She followed those questions by asking why people smoke if it's bad for them. By this point, she was already moving toward the last action of the mind. She had gathered enough information for her to make a choice regarding the value of that action.

If Muḥāsibī is correct that these are the primary actions of the intellect, it is essential to develop educational systems that focus on these areas: language arts, critical thinking, and problem solving. We will describe some of the educational implications of these ideas in more detail in the section on Moral Education.

The Second and Third Levels of the Intellect

Up to this point, we have only explained Muḥāsibī's first level of intellect which simply attempts to establish the innateness of the intellect and its functions. The second and third levels of the intellect, which are closely related to one another, are used throughout the Qur'ān and prophetic narrations.

The second level is *fahm*, correct understanding of things as they truly are. It is the ability to understand all that one hears, touches, tastes, or smells. What is perhaps most critical is that Muḥāsibī points out that all people, whether they are guided to the right path or not, share equally the ability to comprehend meanings. The reason the Arabs used the word *ʿaql* for understanding is that the root meaning of *ʿaql* is to tie something up; when a person has understood something, he has grasped its meaning.

The third meaning is *baṣīrah* (insight), which he calls divine insight, and is discussed at length. He describes this as an intuition into the value of actions, both beneficial and harmful, in the hereafter. This type of *ʿaql* is increased or decreased in accordance with one's esteem and reverence for Allah and in accordance with one's recognition of Allah's blessings upon them. It is by means of *baṣīrah* that one gains protection and safety from divine punishment and enters into divine felicity. *Baṣīrah* also develops reverence for Allah and places within a person the desire to seek knowledge and understanding of ultimate realities. As the person learns and understands more, so too should their recognition of Allah increase, and in turn their desire for His reward and fear of His wrath.

Concluding his breakdown of these three different levels, Muḥāsibī says,

> This is what the intellect is. And whosoever does not possess the last meaning (of the intellect) but has that base level of innate intellect by which Allah has differentiated between the intelligent and the insane, that person does not possess the divine intellect but does possess the intellect of understanding, and so against him, the proof has been established.[23]

Throughout his work, Muḥāsibī emphasizes that the first two levels of the intellect are critical for the development of the third and that upright actions are what truly inform us about the quality and soundness of one's intellect. Regardless of what a person may know, it is ultimately their actions that determine whether they are considered intelligent or not. Muḥāsibī's pragmatic approach to the role of the intellect forces us to include behavioral understanding, regulation, and modification in the definition of intelligence. This is why we have defined emotional intelligence as an essential and fundamental element of the *ʿaql*.

Moral intelligence is slightly different from emotional intelligence in that it involves the capacity to process moral information and to manage self-regulation in such a way that desirable moral ends can

---

23 Muḥāsibī, *Māhiyyat al-ʿAql*, p. 212.

be attained. This definition adequately summarizes what Muḥāsibī calls *ʿaql*. Islamic scholarship did not have to create subcategories of intelligence called moral and social intelligence because it implied that the intelligent individual was the one whose actions were consistent with the logical conclusions of their faith.

Hinting toward the ideal that the intelligent person is one who combines moral, social, and emotional intelligence, Allah says in the Qur'ān,

> . . .and set for him a light by which he walks among men.[24]

According to many commentators, the meaning of the word "light" in this verse is the Qur'ān itself. But what is essential for our discussion is that this verse speaks about social harmony as the ultimate objective of the revelation. We will speak in detail in the coming chapters about the relationship between revelation and the intellect, but at this point, I would simply like readers to recognize that the primary test of intelligence is how one "walks" or lives amongst the people.

Muḥāsibī explains that the intellect is the addressee of divine commands of righteousness. The *ʿaql* is responsible for receiving the revelation and learning how to "walk" correctly. Ghazālī not only adopted the same understanding of the intellect, but he expanded it to show how key aspects of emotional intelligence, such as self-knowledge, are vital elements of prophetic intelligence.

REASON

As a student and teacher of the Islamic sciences for the past seventeen years, I have witnessed an interesting trend among new students to sacred knowledge and the pedagogical tradition around sacred knowledge. Perhaps it was an inspiring lecture that someone heard that awakened within them the desire to study their faith. Perhaps

24 Q 6:122.

it was an overwhelming feeling of shame when one realized their ignorance regarding their own religious identity. Or perhaps it was the cacophony of a troubled heart cut off from its Creator that nagged at a person's conscience until they had no choice but to respond. Whatever the reason, I have seen hundreds of students arrive at the doors of religious institutions with the desire to know Allah and tread the path to Him, only to be confused or even demoralized by the path and direction given to them. The path of study presented is not one of long moments of reflection in solitude or contemplation over the subtleties of Qur'ānic commentaries, but rather one that begins with years of grammar, rhetoric, literature, and morphology.

I can vividly recall the time when I too found myself in this very same predicament. I was a student in a Qur'ān memorization program in a traditional Islamic seminary, working day and night to commit the entire Qur'ān to memory. As I struggled daily to memorize, I found myself deeply desiring to understand the words I was reciting. So, I turned to my teacher for guidance. Shaykh Manṣūr Memon held the position of teaching *Ṣaḥiḥ Muslim.* He was a quiet man; one could easily count his words during a gathering. He grew up in the city of Madinah and studied the Islamic sciences in England and Egypt before moving to Canada where he, along with his father and brothers, worked to open a *madrasah.* His smile was prophetically welcoming, and he was always ready to help any student in need. Our relationship was such that he was confident that I could handle whatever advice he gave me. I sat before him and described my problem. I explained that I wanted to know more and was becoming bored with just memorizing. "Can I study *tafsīr* on the side?" I asked. I can't help but remember the frankness with which he replied, "No!" he said, "The time for that will come."

Shaykh Manṣūr didn't agree to my request because it went against the traditional pedagogical system's structure for academic progression. Like the Ottoman educational system of the 18th century, the *darse-nizāmī* pedagogical system of South Asia is very particular about the curriculum for students of religious knowledge. In regard to curriculum, we find that both traditions (early Ottoman and *darse-nizāmī*) are very flexible and are often modified according to the needs of the time in which they are applied. The *darse-nizāmī* tradition, for example, culminates with students reading the six authentic books of prophetic narrations, known as *Al-Ṣiḥāḥ al-Sittah*. While this is currently viewed as standard practice in many *sunnī madrasahs* around the world, this was not always the case. It was only after Shah Wali Allah al-Dihlawī returned to India after having completed extensive studies in the holy cities of Makkah and Madīnah, that this aspect of the *darse-nizāmī* system, now seen as practically indispensable, was added. What was not very flexible about the system was its emphasis on a gradual progression through an abundance of rational and linguistic study. Both pedagogical systems prohibited students from accessing the primary sources, such as Qur'ān and Hadith literature and the principles of jurisprudence, until one had mastered grammar, rhetoric, and logic. These pedagogical systems implicitly inform us how Muslim scholars viewed the intellect and its relation to religious learning.

It was understood in classical Islamic pedagogy that many people fail to submit to Allah due to the corruption of language and intellect. Thus, anyone seeking to know Allah and be ranked amongst the inheritors of prophethood had to first master language and thought. The classical structure of education in Ottoman *madrasahs* during the reign of Sulayman the Magnificent (1520–1566 CE/ 926–973 AH), as explained by Tashkupri Zada (1560 CE / 967 AH) in his book *Miftāḥ al-Saʿādah wa Miṣbaḥ al-Siyādah,* was divided into three categories: (a) the ancillary sciences also called *ʿulūm Ālah*; (b) the philosophical sciences or *ʿulūm al-ḥikmiya* and (c) the revelatory sciences or *ʿulūm al-shariʿa*. This work serves as a great resource for understanding how Muslims traditionally understood the intersection of the intellect and religion. At the beginning of his first section, Tashkupri Zada provides his readers with a general summary of all knowledge. "Know that all things that exist are on one of four levels: the written, the spoken, the conceptualized, and the material. Each one of these is the means to that which follows it." The Islamic pedagogical obsession with the sciences of language and thinking is because, unlike sensory perception of the material, the intellect must be trained on how to conceptualize, speak, and write.

This same structure still exists in almost all South Asian *madrasahs* and in other places, such as Egypt and Syria. The difficulty faced by most new students who embark on dedicated study of the Islamic tradition is that the first few years of their studies will almost entirely focus on the ancillary sciences. For many, the long hours of rote memorization of verbal scales seem far from the purpose for which they had set out. They would prefer to spend that time sitting reciting the Qur'ān, chanting the name of their Glorious Creator, or better yet, reading something that emotionally moves them towards piety. For a student wishing to know Allah on a deeper, spiritual level, desiring to love Him more and obey Him better, a book on Arabic morphology seems to completely miss the mark.[25]

Language	Critical thinking
Arabic vocabulary (*lughah*) 3 years Arabic morphology (*ṣarf*) 2 years Arabic grammar (*naḥw*) 3–4 years Arabic rhetoric (*balāghah*) 2–3 years Arabic prosody (*ʿarūḍ*) Arabic literature (*adab*) 3 years Linguistic theory (*waḍʿ*) Persian language (*Farsi*)	Logic (*manṭiq*) 2–3 years Dialectics (*al-baḥth wa al-munāẓarah*)

Tashkupri Zada explains that the ancillary sciences were divided into two groups: (a) the sciences that sharpen the tool of language; and (b) the sciences that give one the tools for critical thinking and rational thought. Custodians of prophetic knowledge had to be masters at recognizing and forming sound arguments so that they could present the message of Allah to others. They also had to be masters of articula-

25 Karamali, *The Madrasa Curriculum in Context*, p. 3.

tion in order to communicate the message sufficiently. We are told by Allah that Arabic was chosen as the means of communication for the final message because of its precision and clarity.[26] The single source of pride for the Arabs before the coming of the messenger was that they possessed a very rich language.

Without learning vocabulary and studying grammar and rhetoric, one would be incapable of witnessing the truly miraculous nature of the Qur'ān and understanding its rational arguments. For Muslims, it is considered the primary miracle of Muḥammad ﷺ and, for Muslims and non-Muslims alike, the Qur'ān is an unparalleled literary masterpiece. For this reason, after completing three to four years of vocabulary, morphology, and grammar lessons, seminary students usually spend another two to three years studying complicated books of rhetoric. The objective of studying rhetoric is twofold. On one hand, rhetoric is the primary science needed for one to build a capacity to appreciate the miraculous nature of the Qur'ān. On the other, rhetorical mastery is the tool by which one delivers the message to others. Typically, mastery of rhetoric in classical seminaries meant that one had studied *ʿilm al-maʿānī*, *ʿilm al-bayān*, and *ʿilm al-badīʿ* (*the science of meanings, the science of expression, and the science of rhetorical figures*). The first (*ʿilm al-maʿānī*) focuses on learning how to place words together according to the needs of the situation. The second (*ʿilm al-bayān*) focuses on learning the intended meanings of statements and how meanings are conveyed through words and phrases. The purpose of learning this science is to protect one from specifying or communicating the wrong meaning to one's audience. The last (*ʿilm al-badīʿ*) focuses on the beauty of speech.

After years of ancillary linguistic studies, students were considered only partially developed. In the Qur'ān, Allah tells us that "He teaches by means of the pen." In another verse, Allah swears by "the pen and that which it writes" and an entire Sūrah is titled *The Pen*. One

---

26 Q 26:195.

prophetic narration tells us that the very first thing Allah created was the pen. Once their writing, speech, and articulation were perfected, students were now required to learn *manṭiq*, or logic, the science of correct thought and sound judgment. True faith was considered that which was logical and reasonable and was grounded within a person's heart, not a result of external pressure. Studying logic trains people how to think correctly and is a means for opening people's eyes to the validity of the claims of the prophets. Tashkupri Zada even considered it the most important of the intellectual sciences. He even goes so far as to say that learning logic is an individual religious obligation (*farḍ ʿayn*)—a view that was subject to much criticism in light of the debates surrounding the legality of learning the science.

Logic was also given the name *ʿilm al-mīzān* (literally the science of the balance) because it teaches a person how to differentiate between fallacious arguments and sound judgments. A mind trained in logic can easily decipher between arguments that deserved merit versus those which are incoherent or flawed. The prophets of Allah, who had the responsibility of placing the message before the intellects of humanity, naturally had to possess a profound ability to distinguish the logically sound from the fallacious.

Though less emphasized today, throughout the 1880s at *Dār al-ʿUlūm Deoband* one of the three daily lessons in the first half of the eight-year program was devoted to logic. Why would a *madrasah* devote so much time to this science? The scholars of Islam were given the title of "inheritors of the prophets" by none other than the Prophet Muḥammad ﷺ himself. After the passing of the Prophet ﷺ, the responsibility of preserving, propagating, and defending the message rested upon their shoulders. They would bear the burden of presenting sound, rational arguments for belief before the intellects of humanity. Education in basic logic was not simply reserved for the highly educated religious scholars; rather, Islamic civilization understood that a strong religious community had to holistically master sound thinking. Satan, from the Qur'ānic perspective, was the first to use flawed logic. Upon the creation of Ādam, we are taught that Satan refused to bow down before him. When questioned by Allah, Satan presented arguably the first logically flawed statement.

> I am better than him. You created me of fire while You created him of mud.[27]

He made two false assumptions. First, he made an unfounded assumption that fire is better than clay and secondly, he assumed that one's rank or closeness to Allah is based on factors outside of their actions. Through this story, we are exposed to the devilish nature of irrational thinking.

This brings us to the topic of rationality. What is rationality? While there have been many competing views, a commonly accepted definition of reason and rationality is:

> The systematic and controlling use of beliefs, arguments, or actions based on well-grounded premises and valid arguments such that another person who has access to the same information and can understand the argument correctly ought to agree that the premises are well-grounded, that the logic is sound, and that the resultant beliefs, arguments, or actions are correct.[28]

This definition encompasses many defining ideals of a believer's life. Actions, beliefs, and arguments should be controlled and systematic, not solely emotional. The premises of any claim or argument should be grounded. Lastly, we should deem incorrect those actions that do not fit within the definition of reasonable. Thus, reason provides us with the ability to judge and distinguish what is appropriate from that which is inappropriate.

In *God and Logic in Islam*, John Walbridge explains that this definition provides us with the following core elements of rationality:

---

27 Q 7:12.

28 Waldbridge, *God and Logic in Islam*, p. 16.

1. Well-grounded premises;
2. Sound logic; and
3. Systematic and controlled resort to reason.

Returning to the question of why seminaries would focus so much time on logic, Peter Kreeft, author of *Socratic Logic,* argues that logic is an "aid and ally to faith."[29] He explains that while faith can go beyond logic, it must never contradict it.

It is interesting to note that one of the many benefits of learning logic, according to Peter Kreeft, is that sound logic helps one recognize their own rational limits; that is, a mind trained in logic knows when to stop and what lies beyond the scope of the rational.

One of the first complete Arabic textbooks on logic written in South Asia was *Sullam al-ʿUlūm* by Muḥibballāh al-Bihārī. Though concise and undated, this textbook begins by highlighting the very same "limiting" function of logic. Biḥārī starts his book, like all other classical Islamic works, by praising Allah while connecting that praise to the subject matter of the book. For example, works on the governing principles of law would beautifully praise Allah for giving humanity a code by which to live and thank Allah for providing humanity with a *sharīʿah*. Biḥārī's *Sullam* similarly begins, "Glory be to Him, how great is He who cannot be defined or conceptualized!" For many commentators, these phrases *lā yuḥaddu* (cannot be defined) and *lā yutaṣawwaru* (cannot be conceptualized) were the subjects of many lengthy discussions. This is because the first law of logic is to conceptualize (define), discern a premise's facticity, and finally to determine if a conclusion is sound based on the terms and premises. Biḥārī writes, "Knowledge is conceptualization." What Biḥārī does through his opening is highlight exactly what Kreeft has stated: logic allows us to know our limitations. This is important because it provides us the ability to recognize the *super-rational*. We can use our intellect to

29 Kreeft, *Socratic Logic,* p. 4.

come close to the Divine and to know that He exists, but that is the limit of the intellect.

This brief look at the emphasis placed on grammar, logic, and rhetoric within Islamic seminaries throughout history is meant to show that Islamic pedagogical thought considered sound reasoning and articulation as the basis for a strong religious community. Rationality was not the enemy of the theist, as Locke and Spinoza would opine. On the contrary, the immaterial soul was of divine origin, and rationality was its defining attribute. Rationality is the strongest ally to belief in Allah and His prophets.

11
Emotional Intelligence

EMOTIONAL AND SOCIAL INTELLIGENCE: TWO PARTS OF THE *ʿAQL*

"He who mixes with the people and is patient with them is better than the one who avoids the people and doesn't have patience with them."[30] Human interaction is amazingly complex, as we all play multiple roles in the lives of those around us. We are fathers and mothers, brothers and sisters, and sons and daughters at the same time. One's inability to live up to the responsibilities that come with these various roles deeply affects the greater society. Young children without righteous caregivers as role models threaten the fabric of our collective moral codes. Fruitful and positive interaction is dependent upon emotional understanding. Therefore, the Qur'ānic emphasis on following the example of the Prophet ﷺ demands that every Muslim strive to become an expert in emotional awareness and understanding. Take, for example, the narrations that speak about the rights of one's neighbors. We are told in one narration that if a person is cooking food, and their neighbors smell it, then they are strongly encouraged to share that food, even if they must water it down to do so. In a well-

30 Ibn Māja, *Sunan Ibn Māja*, vol. 5, p. 160.

known narration, the Prophet ﷺ taught us, "All of you are shepherds (tending to your flock), and all of you will be questioned regarding your treatment of that flock."[31] One cannot expect to treat their flock well if they cannot understand them.

Emotional and social intelligence are essential elements of the *ʿaql* because they teach us how to help, guide, and engage with everyone around us. They make us ideal shepherds. Healthy relationships require a perceptive emotional understanding and large amount of emotional investment. Without these two factors, our most precious ties of kinship and friendships will dry up and wither away. The care and attention required for healthy relationships is described in a narration of the Prophet ﷺ,

> Indeed, the family of my father are not my protectors. Rather my close protectors are only Allah and the righteous believers. They (the family of my father) have a bond of kinship with me that I keep damp.[32]

Commenting on this narration, Badr al-Dīn al-ʿAynī explains that the use of the word damp here refers to the natural tendency for things to crack, break, or die when they lose all their moisture.[33] He says the word *balal,* which is used in the narration, is also the word used for dew, which preserves life. The Prophet ﷺ is explaining to us that some effort has to be made to preserve kinship's inherent moisture, or else the bonds of kinship will dry up and break. Emotional investment in the lives of those closest to us is how we maintain the moisture needed for healthy relationships.

As a husband and father of three young children, I have grown to understand and appreciate the miraculous nature of the Prophet Muḥammad's ﷺ complete emotional investment in the lives of those he interacted with. When Ghazālī says that there was no one more

31 Muslim, *Ṣaḥīḥ Muslim*, vol. 3, p. 1459.

32 Bukhari, *Kitāb al-Ādāb*, Ch. 14 #5990.

33 ʿAyni, *ʿUmdat al-Qārī*, vol. 22, p. 147.

intelligent than the Prophet Muḥammad ﷺ, we should focus on his ability to understand his own emotions and those of others, as well as his ability to positively influence the emotional state of everyone around him. The perfection of this type of intelligence is described in a beautiful narration which describes the Prophet's ﷺ manners on various occasions. Ḥusayn ibn ʿAli said, "I asked my father about the gatherings of the Messenger of Allah." He said, "The Messenger of Allah would not stand or sit except with the remembrance of Allah. When he would go to a people, he would sit wherever there was space available, and he would order others to do the same. He would give every attendee his due portion of attention, to such an extent that every attendee would think that there was no one more noble in the sight of the Prophet ﷺ than himself."[34] This narration shows that the Companions noticed how consistently and thoroughly the Prophet ﷺ emotionally invested in those enjoying his company. Anyone occupying space with him felt valued, important, and special. They didn't have to go out of their way to seek his attention; their presence alone was enough to make them worthy of it. If this type of emotional investment in people is intrinsically part of the prophetic model of intellect, then we are forced to question some of the dominant cultural understandings of what it means to be masculine.

When we study his emotional intelligence, we begin to appreciate the sharpness of his intrapersonal and interpersonal emotional awareness and understanding. His keen awareness and understanding were the primary factors that led to his skills in emotion management. We will see that his emotional intelligence was a tool for change, and it all began with emotional investment in those around him. He was a compassionate father, friend, and husband, who was neither afraid to cry when he was hurt nor insecure in showing his feelings. He showed his community that when revelation is combined with the *ʿaql,* it provides a person with the ability to not only look into the depths of

34 Tirmidhī, *Shamāʾil al-Tirmidhī,* Hadith #365.

their own hearts and minds but into those of others as well. The ability and willingness to be in touch with one's own feelings and the feelings of others is based on empathy. It is empathy for one's own self which becomes the basis of intrapersonal intelligence, and empathy for others which becomes the basis of interpersonal intelligence, both of which are key aspects of emotional intelligence and prophetic influence.

In order to build this aspect of intelligence within his companions, he began by deconstructing the incorrect manifestations of masculinity that existed in his community. Historical accounts indicate that his society placed little to no value on male emotionality. He introduced his community to aspects of male emotionality that were typically frowned upon and considered unmanly. He showed them through practical example that to publicly display one's feelings was not only normal but a sign of Allah's mercy. His hyper-sensitive awareness and understanding of people's feelings constituted the core of his influence. As a result, he was mocked and ridiculed and rumors of the Prophet ﷺ who publicly showed affection for his children spread across the Arabian peninsula. Despite this, he continued to be true to this aspect of prophetic intelligence and did not give in to the pressures of the ignorant. Seldom do people possess the emotional bandwidth to handle their own problems and worries, let alone those of others. We naturally avoid pain, and for this reason, many people shy away from emotional investment in others altogether. In the Qur'ān, Allah explains that the Prophet's ﷺ deepest pain was knowing that others were in pain. In other words, he was so deeply invested in the lives of those around him that he shared their pain.

> There has come to you a Messenger from among yourselves, grievous to whom is your suffering, concerned for you, to the believers gentle and compassionate.[35]

35 Q 9:128.

EMOTIONAL INTELLIGENCE: A TOOL FOR CHANGE

Why do we consider emotional intelligence to be half of the prophetic intellect? The answer lies in the word "messenger." Messengers of Allah are tasked with the divine responsibility of conveying to humanity the keys to their salvation. They are not only tasked with passing on the message but also with being a living example of that message. When ʿĀ'isha, the wife of the Prophet ﷺ, was asked to explain the character of the blessed Prophet ﷺ, her reply was, "His character was the Qur'ān."[36] We are giving emotional intelligence a place of primacy in the construct of prophetic intelligence because it seems implausible that Allah would send a messenger without providing that messenger with the means necessary to exemplify and transmit the message to others. If the prophets of Allah did not have the necessary knowledge and skills needed to successfully pass on the message to the next generation, the argument would be incomplete. People could easily excuse themselves of all accountability because the message was never conveyed.

We also see clear examples in the Qur'ān that this knowledge was being perpetually perfected in the character of the Prophet ﷺ. Slight slips in his emotional intelligence were rare but when they did occur, Allah gently addressed the mistake by means of revelation. Allah says in the Qur'ān, "If you (O Muḥammad) were harsh and hardhearted, then the people would flee from you." This verse clearly placed the burden of keeping an audience upon the shoulders of the Prophet ﷺ .What this means is that the Prophet ﷺ had to be aware of what would push people away; he had to know what would create cognitive and emotional barriers to receptivity. When we study the *shamā'il* (books about his character), we find that he was beyond exceptional in his ability to make people receptive. He took great care in studying the people around him and deeply understanding them. Only after the Prophet ﷺ had exhausted all the means of removing barriers to

36 Bayhaqī, *Shuʿab al-Īmān*, vol. 3, p. 23.

receptivity would the responsibility to affirm the message be shifted to those called to it.

Another example of this prophetic responsibility can be found in the story of Prophet Mūsā when he was commissioned to call Pharaoh and the children of Israel to Allah. When Allah informed him of the task he was chosen for, he immediately attempted to excuse himself because he had a slight speech impediment. He knew that his speech impediment could potentially affect the receptivity of people to the message. He felt that this disqualified him from being a prophet. He also felt that the act of manslaughter he committed might come between the people and guidance. All of these examples show that Allah's prophets understood that many factors can affect a person's receptivity to learning something new, especially when the implications of that new information call into question almost every aspect of a person's identity. History tells us that initially, people did not accept the message of the Prophet Muḥammad ﷺ; they completely rejected him and accused him of being a liar.

One particular incident shows very clearly that he ﷺ understood how necessary it was for him to remove any cognitive or emotional barriers that existed between him and his community. When the people of his hometown of Makkah had almost completely rejected him, he felt that it was time to turn his attention to a neighboring town. The city of Ṭā'if was a major city, and the Prophet ﷺ was hopeful that perhaps they would be receptive to the message. Unfortunately, they completely rejected him and refused to even listen to what he had to say. They chased him out of town, throwing stones at him until his injuries left him completely covered in blood. Barely making it outside the city, the Prophet ﷺ collapsed. Too weak to move, he turned his attention to his Lord and made one of the most powerful supplications made by a prophet of Allah.

> O Allah, only to You do I complain about my lack of strength, my insufficient strategies, and lowliness in the sight of the people. You

> are my Lord. To whom do you turn me over? Someone distant from me who will forsake me? Or have you placed my affair in the hands of my enemy?[37]

The Prophet ﷺ felt that he was the reason why people were not accepting the message. His concern regarding "low status in the eyes of the people" informs us that he understood that people naturally judge the seriousness of a message based on the stature of the message bearer. The people of Ṭā'if were extremely ignorant, so much so that they adamantly refused to engage in any dialogue. In reality, this was not due to any shortcoming of the Prophet ﷺ; he demonstrated the best of character and displayed extreme patience in the face of such ignorance. But the beginning of the supplication teaches us what he was focused on: making sure that he was not the reason why someone did not accept the message.

Because his message was not geographically restricted like that of other prophets, those who inherited the message would have the extra burden of transferring the message to a people with whom they were unfamiliar. The intelligence needed to pass the message of the Prophet Muḥammad ﷺ around the world included an understanding of the cultural differences between people. Without this understanding, effective communication and passing on of his message would be impossible.

A sharp emotional intelligence is built upon the development of both intra and interpersonal intelligence. These intelligences are the backbone of EQ, and they provide a person with an emotional awareness and understanding of his or her own self, an empathic understanding of others, and the ability needed to communicate effectively and cause change. Emotional intelligence by itself is not sufficient for individual reform or societal reform; instead, it is only one part of the puzzle. The *ʿaql* or intellect that is referenced repeatedly in the Qur'ān is a more comprehensive tool that not only recognizes

---

37 Ibn Kathīr, *al-Bidāya wa al-Nihāya*, vol. 3, p. 136.

how to understand the psychological and emotional aspects of people but recognizes morally upright and sound behavior. Thereafter, this intellect, if healthy and mature, forces a person to conform to that standard. Therefore, we understand the *ʿaql* to be a comprehensive collection of intelligences analogous to Howard Gardner's Multiple Intelligences theory.

Taking into consideration the considerable diversity found within Western Muslim communities, we see how both moral and emotional intelligence are needed. Fostering and nurturing healthy communities require that we understand how people receive our messages. This is the interpersonal intelligence aspect of EQ. Without grounding the moral component of our community, diversity can lead to what some contemporary moral theorists call moral plasticity, a phenomenon where concrete understandings of good and evil, right and wrong, are lost. Moral education (which will be discussed throughout the book) involves building a morally intelligent heart focused on correcting the message that we are communicating to the world; in other words, moral intelligence helps us maintain our ideals and live by them, while emotional intelligence ensures that the message is effectively communicated to others.

Interpersonal understanding is the core of emotional intelligence. My father would often tell me, "It's not what you say, son; it's what they hear." From the perspective of emotional intelligence, this statement is very accurate. The way we interpret words, body language, verbal inflections, and facial expressions is based on many different factors. The subtle power of this book lies in the simple fact that your emotional intelligence is the primary agent of change and thus, the most powerful force you have. You must understand how people perceive what you are communicating to them. What is missing from my father's statement is the primacy of moral intelligence. Throughout this book, I attempt to show how the Prophet Muḥammad ﷺ demonstrated a level of perfection of both of these intelligences.

EMOTIONAL AWARENESS: INTRAPERSONAL AWARENESS OR SELF-KNOWLEDGE

What exactly is emotional awareness? Howard Gardner divided emotional awareness into two skills or intelligences: *intra-* and *interpersonal* intelligence. They involve the capacity to notice moods, temperaments, motivations, and intentions in one's self (intra) and in others (inter) as well. Perfecting the *ʿaql* demands that one develops acute intra and interpersonal emotional awareness because other emotional intelligence capacities, such as emotion regulation, are dependent upon first being aware of emotional changes. It is also this awareness that communicates to others our level of concern for them and their well-being.

Ghazālī begins his *Alchemy of Happiness*, a book on spiritual reformation, with a chapter dedicated to the topic of *maʿrifat al-Nafs* or knowledge of one's self. In emotional intelligence training, self-knowledge is considered to be not only an essential *means* for understanding and influencing the emotional states of others, but also the only means by which a person can gain control of themselves. We fail to realize that there is a high price to pay for ignoring our own emotional states. Feelings and desires that have not been acknowledged and examined will continue to haunt us and affect our behavior until we face them and deal with them appropriately. By ignoring our emotions, we slowly develop a lack of familiarity with ourselves and this lack of familiarity leads to avoiding moments of inner reflection and contemplation. We feel awkward when we are alone, just as one feels awkward in the presence of a stranger; we have effectively become strangers to ourselves. Ghazālī explains that true knowledge of anything outside of the human being can only be obtained after one has understood themselves completely.

According to Ghazālī's *Alchemy of Happiness*, true bliss and contentment ultimately develop from gaining a deep gnosis of Allah. Connecting people to Allah is the fundamental goal of revelation and the purpose of worship. This bliss and contentment, however, cannot come until one has freed themselves from the control of their own desires and passions. So long as you are controlled by your lower self, you can never rise above the level of beasts. Allah eloquently explains the tendency for people to succumb to the whims and lowly passions of the self in the Qur'ān,

> And had We willed We could have raised him by means of them [the signs], but he clung to the earth and followed his passions. There his likeness is as the likeness of a dog. . .[38]

Ghazālī says, "Strive to know thyself so that you may discover the path to Allah and gaze upon His splendor. Break away the shackles of passion and anger. . .Allah did not create these things within you for you to be controlled by them, but rather for you to control them."[39] It is no wonder that the Prophet ﷺ warned his followers so much about the evils that lie within. The true reality is that these passions and desires are not evil when controlled and guided. But when they are left unchecked, they take control and lead a person to self-destruction. Knowledge of the self is the first step in developing self-control. It should not be seen as a goal in and of itself, but rather as a means to the ultimate goal of self-control and upright behavior.

Thus, self-knowledge has a tactical importance for the spiritual well-being of humanity, from the Qur'ānic and prophetic perspective. The lower self is one of the enemies of the soul so long as the *ʿaql* is unaware of its tricks and schemes. As the Arabic saying states, "A man is an enemy to that which he is ignorant of." Before the lower self is cultured and trained, it is considered an accomplice of the three other enemies of man, namely the devil, one's desires, and love of the immediate. Shaykh Aḥmadou Bamba, a Senegalese scholar and spiritual guide of millions, was imprisoned by French colonialists because of his overwhelming influence on hundreds of thousands of

38 Q 7:176.

39 Ghazālī, *The Alchemy of Happiness*, p. 14.

his followers who closely adhered to his guidance. He was a master of many Islamic sciences and wrote works in various fields but is perhaps most well-known for his poems regarding the science of *taṣawwuf*.

In one of his works, he writes that the enemies of man lie within the word *nashhadu*, literally translated as "we bear witness." Shaykh Bamba was referring to the four Arabic letters that comprise this word, each of which represents one of the enemies. The letter *nūn* represents *nafs* or lower self, *shīn* represents *shayṭān* or the devil, *hā* represents *hawā* or desires, and *dāl* represents *dunyā* or love of the immediate. Obtaining knowledge of the self is so difficult that the Prophet ﷺ called it the *jihād al-akbar*, or the greatest struggle. The lower self is only an enemy to man when it is left unchecked by the *ʿaql*. Otherwise, when kept within its boundaries, it serves as a valuable aid for our well-being. It is an indispensable tool given to us by Allah. By now we begin to see how the approaches of Muḥāsibī and Ghazālī, which consider the *ʿaql* to be a manager and regulator of actions, fit very well with the function of intrapersonal emotional intelligence, a topic we will discuss in detail in following sections.

INTERPERSONAL EMOTIONAL AWARENESS: WE ARE WIRED TO CONNECT

"He is pained by that which hurts you." Describing the Blessed Prophet ﷺ in the Qur'ān, Allah highlights an aspect of his character that formed the cornerstone of his ability to transform the world and become one of the most influential leaders the world has ever known. Only after understanding people can one positively motivate them, and this can only be done when one recognizes the value of emotionally investing in those around them. This one verse, "He is pained by that which hurts you," tells us that at the core of our beloved Prophet's heart was the desire to relieve the emotional and mental suffering of humanity. He allowed himself to care so much about others that he himself was deeply troubled by the slightest discomfort of those around him. We cannot study the emotional intelligence of the Prophet ﷺ without first appreciating the great empathy he had for Allah's creation.

In his *Mawāhib,* Qasṭallānī mentioned a statement of Suhrawardī that explains, with vivid detail, precisely why Qāḍī 'Iyāḍ and others felt that the Prophet Muḥammad ﷺ was the most intelligent of all creation.

Suhrawardī said:

> Whoever contemplates the Prophet's excellent management of the Arabs—who were like wild and scattered beasts, with repulsive and aloof natures—and how he led them and bore patiently with their boorishness and harms until they began to follow him and rally under him and fight against their own families and fathers and sons for his sake, and how they preferred him over their own selves and emigrated from their homelands and beloveds for his pleasure. All this despite him not having prior experience, and despite him not reading books from which the narratives of the past nations could have been learned. Indeed, if you contemplate these things, you will come to the realization that he is the most intelligent of all creation! And because his intellect is the most expansive of intellects, it should come as no surprise that his noble qualities of character were comprehensive and unlimited.[40]

This statement completely encompasses the modern understanding of multiple intelligences. True intelligence is no longer a simple IQ, but rather a combination of the three aforementioned intelligences and influence.

Anyone who has lived with a loved one addicted to drugs or alcohol, worked in the social sector, or simply had to walk through underprivileged neighborhoods will appreciate the skill, knowledge and understanding of human character necessary to bring about the likes of the moral revolution that took place during the mission of the Prophet Muḥammad ﷺ. We read book after book about love,

40 Qasṭallānī, *al-Mawāhib al-Ladunniyyah*, vol. 2, p. 325.

relationships, and developing managerial skills because we understand that, at the end of the day, what really matters is our ability to connect with the people around us.

The rate at which Muslims are leaving Islam is a testimony to our loss of interpersonal understanding.[41] As we study the science of emotional intelligence through the lens of the prophetic model, we see that his personal interactions with others starts with sincere empathy, thereby necessitating an emotional investment. This emotional investment later developed within him a keen awareness and understanding of the emotions of others. That emotional understanding allowed him to deeply connect with everyone that he met. It also allowed him to remove any emotional barriers that could potentially prevent his message from being received.

A profound example of the Prophet's ability to connect with everyone around him can be witnessed in an incident that took place between him and ʿAmr ibn al-ʿĀṣ, who had just returned from a reconnaissance mission. He was handpicked by the blessed Prophet ﷺ for this mission and was going directly to the Prophet ﷺ to update him. After informing the Prophet ﷺ about completing his mission, he felt the need to ask a question that had been in his heart for some time. As we mentioned earlier, the Prophet ﷺ had this amazing ability to make everyone who sat in his presence feel as if they were the most beloved to him. In this moment, ʿAmr felt that he held a special place in the heart of the Prophet ﷺ, and he wanted verbal confirmation of this. So, before leaving his presence, he asked, "O Prophet of Allah! Who do you love the most?"

"ʿĀ'isha," replied the Prophet of Allah ﷺ.

"I mean, who from the men do you love the most?"

"Her father."

41 A Pew Study on the percentage of American Muslims who no longer identify as Muslims is 23%; another Pew study also informs us that the rate of conversion into Islam is 23% as well. http://www.pewresearch.org/fact-tank/2018/01/26/the-share-of-americans-who-leave-islam-is-offset-by-those-who-become-muslim/

"Then, who?"

"Umar."

"Then who?"

They went back-and-forth until ʿAmr stopped asking out of fear that he would find out his true level. How was one man able to make an entire city feel as if he loved each of them more than anyone else? We, on the other hand, struggle to make our small families of two, three, or four people feel loved and connected to us. We have lost this knowledge and forgotten how much our beloved role model emotionally invested in everyone around him. He was connected to everyone around him. That connection was felt by all who shared space with him. Interpersonal awareness includes primal empathy, attunement, empathetic accuracy, and social cognition, concepts that we will revisit later in this section. These capacities enable a person to sense the inner states of others and to understand their thoughts and feelings. But awareness is not enough; one must also smoothly and effectively interact with those who they have just emotionally understood. This involves synchronizing with the nonverbal emotional signals and presenting oneself correctly.

As we will see in more detail, the unlettered Prophet Muḥammad ﷺ was blessed with a heightened level of interpersonal intelligence. He taught that the *ʿaql* or intellect is a "light by which one walks among men."[42] He understood that the word *emotion* contains within it the word *motion,* and that emotion offers human beings a distinctive readiness for action. Emotions are what bring out the best and worst of us all. What takes place when two people spend considerable time with one another? According to Daniel Goleman, "our brains engage in an emotional tango, a dance of feelings"[43] and these interactions are like modulators that "constantly reset key aspects of our brain's functions" as they orchestrate our emotions. We need to interact with

42 Q 6:122.

43 Goleman, *Social intelligence*, p. 5.

other humans in order to survive. We are designed to be connected with others. Goleman also mentions that recent studies have shown how the feelings generated from these interactions have a ripple effect throughout the entire body.

Developing interpersonal intelligence begins with primal empathy. Empathy is the primary quality that violent criminals lack. Psychopaths (also known as sociopaths) are unable to feel empathy or compassion, which disorients their moral compass and strips them of shame and conscience. Attempting to develop interpersonal intelligence in his community, the Prophet ﷺ had to awaken within them their capacity for primal empathy. They had to learn how to feel with others. Once a young man came to the Prophet Muḥammad ﷺ and asked for permission to fornicate, a major sin in Islam. The Prophet ﷺ worked to develop and fine-tune his moral compass by first developing his capacity to think empathically. He asked the young man if he had a mother or a sister, to which the young man replied that he did. The Prophet ﷺ thereafter encouraged him to feel the pain of someone else. He asked him how he would feel if someone fornicated with his mother. Judging by the disgust expressed by the young man, it seems that he had never thought of his actions from any perspective other than his own. The young man replied that he would hate the thought of anyone fornicating with his mother or sister. After this dialogue with the Prophet ﷺ, the young man said that there was no sin more distasteful to him than fornication. Thus, his moral compass had been calibrated, and his desire to commit this sin was quieted by empathetic contemplation.

Emotional detachment is a characteristic of violent criminals, sexual predators, and abusers. Sexual abusers find enjoyment only when they have completely built up a wall to empathy. They deny, misinterpret, or ignore the natural human tendency to sense others' feelings. They take physical intimacy, one of the most emotionally fulfilling experiences, and strip it of all emotional meaning, thereby making it solely about self-gratification instead of an expression of the highest degree of empathy. Every touch and kiss between a loving married couple should be intended to emotionally stimulate each other.

I am reminded of a sister whom I shall call Zainab to protect her identity. She was married to a young man named Abdullah during her undergraduate years in college. She said that when they started to get to know each other, "Abdullah was the most generous and caring person. He was handsome and charming; he seemed like the perfect husband." Zainab's parents agreed to the marriage, and the two were married. Five years later, they were divorced. Zainab described the final straw that broke the camel's back thus: "Throughout the marriage, he insisted on doing certain sexual actions that made me uncomfortable. I wanted to be a good wife to him, so I went along with it. But one day something happened that told me I had to get out of the marriage. One evening before being intimate, I told him that I was in pain and could not have sex. To that, he coldly replied, 'That's your problem!' At that point, I knew this marriage had to end." What happened to Abdullah? What made him reach this point where the pain of his wife meant nothing to him if it obstructed his pleasure?

The prevalent cultural misunderstanding of masculinity must be corrected and replaced with the prophetic standard of masculinity. It must be corrected by the prophetic model used to correct the young man who wanted permission to fornicate. We must learn to feel empathy again.

After primal empathy has been developed, the next stage of interpersonal awareness is attunement. Sincere, sustained presence facilitates rapport, which is the primary element needed between two people communicating with one another. The beauty of deep listening is that it requires that the listener become attuned to the feelings of the person before them. They must listen beyond the words of the person and be attuned to the inner motivations of the heart. While the primary objective of every teacher is to pass on information to the heart of their students, effective teachers know that students are unreceptive to their teachers until rapport is built. A student becomes receptive to a teacher only after a teacher is able to show presence with the student's inner state. The best teachers are those who listen well. The best therapists are those who are so present with their patients that they connect on a kinesthetic and emotional level. They can create an unbroken feeling of connectedness and provide their patients with a reciprocal effect of every emotion or state the patient experiences. Looking at the Prophet's life, we find many examples of his ability to be attuned to those around him. He could hear the subtle movements within those around him as clearly as others hear that which is verbalized.

Imagine you walk into your house after a long day at work. Today was an exceptionally stressful day due to a misunderstanding that took place between you and a co-worker. You sense that you are still on edge from the stress at work. As you walk in the door, you say *"Bismillah, al-Salām ʿalaykum,"* emulating the way the Prophet ﷺ entered his house. Your spouse has arrived home before you and has begun to prepare some food. Your son comes running down the stairs full of energy; he just turned five years old, and today, he learned how to read a new word from his list of sight words. There is nothing more special to him right now than sharing this with you and making you proud. "Daddy! Daddy!" he screams, running towards you, "Let me show you the new word I learned!" You're exhausted and still on edge, but you consciously choose to ignore your irritation and display intense interest in his words. You drop your bag right there at the door and scoop him up, realizing that rejecting him at this moment, just because you had a bad day, would be devastating to him. For the next five minutes, he slowly reads the new word to you as you pay close attention, smiling and letting him read and figure it out by himself.

This example shows, first and foremost, your own intrapersonal awareness. You had the ability to acknowledge your agitated state from a third-person perspective. You were then able to recognize the cause of that agitation. Then we see your interpersonal intelligence beginning with primal empathy. You read your son's body language and accurately understood the importance of this moment from his perspective. Thereafter you attuned yourself to him and gave undistracted and sustained presence. As you continue to build rapport, this young boy will accept your guidance as he grows. You have connected with him.

The early pioneer in multiple intelligence theory, Howard Gardner, explains in his book, *Frames of Mind,* that, "In its most elementary form, interpersonal intelligence entails the capacity of the young child to discriminate among the individuals around him and to detect their various moods."[44] One of the signs of a child's healthy mental development is that around the age of two, they begin to recognize pain and joy in others around them. Before that age, most children simply don't have the cognitive ability to sense pain in others. This is the most basic level of interpersonal intelligence. I cannot count the number of times my two-year-old son Qāsim has smacked his mother or me as hard as he possibly could while playing. This is because he does not realize that the pain he feels can be felt by others as well. But as our children grow and develop, we teach them to recognize pain in other people by comparing it to their own pain.

So, what does an acute interpersonal intelligence look like? The story we began this section with gives an example of a father who was able to be aware of, or "see," the emotional state, and hence need, of his five-year-old son. His awareness of his own emotional state was the first step towards not allowing his emotions to interfere with displaying the attention his son needed. According to Gardner, the higher levels of interpersonal intelligence are described as "levels that allow a person to read deeply into the intentions of those around them."[45] In an advanced form, interpersonal intelligence permits a skilled adult to read the intentions and desires—even when these have been hidden—of many other individuals and, potentially, to act upon this

---

44 Gardner, *Frames of Mind: The Theory of Multiple Intelligences*, p. 253.

45 Ibid.

knowledge. We will discuss this in more detail in the next section regarding emotional understanding.

It is only natural that Allah would imbue the Prophet Muḥammad ﷺ with an extraordinary capacity for interpersonal intelligence because he, like all the other prophets, was tasked with communicating to people a message of guidance and salvation. A person's ability to effectively communicate with others is dependent upon their ability to connect with others and his or her cultural and emotional understanding of those they are addressing. And just as conveying a message requires a common language, it is also dependent upon recognizing and removing any type of barrier that may prevent a correct understanding of the message. Describing the role and responsibility of the prophets, Allah says, "And We never sent a messenger except with the language of his people, that he might make [the message] clear for them."[46]

We can now see why interpersonal intelligence was part and parcel of prophethood. In light of our understanding of the importance of interpersonal intelligence for communicators, it would seem that this verse is actually telling us that every prophet possessed a deep interpersonal understanding of his people. They were aware of and understood the motivations, intentions, and feelings of their people.

It should be clear by now that the utility of this awareness and intelligence is not found solely in one's ability to be an effective influencer. Stability, trust, and communication within our families are completely dependent upon this intelligence. The wife of the Prophet ﷺ, Umm Salamah, gives us an example of the emotional awareness of her husband. "While I was lying down with the Prophet of Allah under a single woolen sheet, I suddenly got my menses. So, I slipped away as discreetly as possible from under the cover, and I changed into the clothes which I normally wore during my menses. The Prophet ﷺ then said to me: 'Have your menses started?' 'Yes,' I replied. He then asked me to rejoin him under the blanket and lie down close to

46 Q 14: 4.

him. So, I came back and lay down with him under the cover."[47] This narration provides an example for male followers of the Prophet ﷺ to be exceptionally perceptive about the changes their spouses experience. In this example, we see that perception alone is not enough. The Prophet ﷺ verbally confirmed that he noticed what his wife was experiencing, showing his mental awareness and presence. Verbal confirmation informs the other person that you are aware of what they are going through. This verbal confirmation leaves no trace of doubt in the other person's mind you are completely present with them, mentally and emotionally. Lastly, we see that he asked her to come back and lie close to him. This last subtle gesture of love must have had an immensely positive effect on the psyche of Umm Salamah, conveying to her that his love was unconditional and constant. He was not going to distance himself from her because of the change in her state of ritual cleanliness, nor was he going to deprive her of the affection, love, and closeness that she needed from her husband. Many husbands fail miserably in this area, showing a lot of affection and love when their wife is not menstruating, and then completely ignoring her when she is. The Prophet ﷺ understood that Umm Salamah may have needed his love and affection even more so in this vulnerable moment, and he dispelled any negative thoughts that could have been in her mind about her uncleanliness.

In an even more explicit example, we see him demonstrating his emotional awareness to his wife. Joking with his wife ʿĀ'isha, he once said, "I can tell when you are pleased with me and when you are annoyed with me." She, seemingly amused by her husband's statement, replied, "How can you tell?" "When you are happy with me, you often say, 'I swear by the Lord of Muḥammad.' However, when you are upset, you say, 'I swear by the Lord of Ibrāhīm.'" ʿĀ'isha, pleased with her husband's deep understanding of her, replied, "Yes (you are right), O Messenger of Allah, but by Allah, I only leave out your name." There

47 Ibn Māja, *Sunan Ibn Māja*, vol. 1, p. 209.

can be no greater feeling than to know that your spouse attends to and understands your emotional cues. Imagine ʿĀ'isha's feeling of being appreciated and loved as he described her own idiosyncrasies to her. The Prophet ﷺ was showing his wife that he paid close attention to even her subtlest actions. Perhaps even she herself was unaware of this habit until he described it, as it is often the case that we are not aware of the things we say and do in moments of joy and anger. The closer friends and spouses are to one another, the more they not only notice each other's quirky idiosyncrasies, but they begin to unintentionally imitate those idiosyncrasies themselves. It is related that Fāṭimah, the daughter of the Prophet ﷺ resembled the Prophet ﷺ increasingly in appearance, speech, and even gait as she aged.

A common problem that occurs in many relationships is that one person expects the other to have developed a deep understanding of them. Explicit explanations are necessary for those who haven't spent much time together, but close friends, spouses, and family members who have spent considerable time together are often expected to understand emotional changes intuitively. A lack of awareness or understanding communicates to the other person a lack of connection and often leads to larger arguments and frustrated exchanges with one party saying something along the lines of, "Why don't you just tell me?" only to hear the common reply, "Well if I have to tell you then it doesn't matter anymore!"

The Prophet Muḥammad ﷺ said,

> Indeed, Iblīs established his throne upon the water. Then he sent out his troops. Those who are closest to him are those who cause the most turmoil. One of them came to him saying, "I did this and that." Iblīs responded by saying, "You didn't do much." Then another came and said, "I persisted with one man until I created a rift between him and his wife." Iblīs brought him close and embraced him saying, "You did excellent!"[48]

48 Muslim, *Ṣaḥīḥ Muslim*, vol. 4, p. 2167.

Throughout this book, as we explore the emotional intelligence of the Prophet ﷺ, readers will notice many examples of his emotional awareness. This is because all higher levels of emotional intelligence are dependent on emotional awareness. It is the fundamental level of interpersonal intelligence. Miraculously, the Prophet's ﷺ interpersonal emotional awareness was not limited to an awareness of only human emotional changes. We find narrations suggesting a much broader awareness within his heart. There is a narration[49] by a Companion named Yaʿlā ibn Murrah in which he relates a miracle he witnessed at the hands of the Prophet ﷺ. He says that one day he was traveling with the Prophet ﷺ when they passed by a camel that was being used to water crops. When the camel saw the Prophet ﷺ, it began to make a deep grunting sound over and over as if it was calling to the Prophet ﷺ. As the Prophet ﷺ approached, the camel lowered its head to the ground before him. Standing above the camel, touching it gently, the Prophet asked, "Where is the owner of this camel?" When the owner came, the Prophet ﷺ said to him, "Sell me this camel." "No, it is a gift for you, O Prophet of Allah," replied the owner. Realizing the magnitude of the gift he was offering, he immediately followed up, saying, "It is our only camel and a means of our livelihood." "Well, if this is the case and you have no other camel, then know that this camel has just told me that you work it too hard and feed it too little. So be good to it." Another narration states that when the camel saw the Prophet ﷺ, it not only began to grunt and groan but also cried. As the Prophet ﷺ approached it, he placed his hand on the camel, and it immediately became calm.

As we develop interpersonal emotional awareness within ourselves, people who are in pain will, like this camel, call out for help. Many other people passed by this camel, but it either didn't call out for help, or they did not understand its calls for help. If it didn't call out to anyone else, the question must be asked, "What did it see in

49 Tabrīzī, *Mishkāt al-Maṣābīh,* vol. 3, p. 1664.

Muḥammad ﷺ that it didn't in see in others?" Did it see a prophet of Allah upon whom the speech of Allah was revealed? Or did it sense the vastness of the man's heart passing by it? Whatever the case may be, the camel recognized that the man in front of it could understand its pain, so it called for help. As we try to increase our emotional awareness and understanding, people who are in pain will sense our awareness and understanding, and they will call out to us just as this camel called out to the Prophet ﷺ. The emotionally 'woke' heart must then choose to respond or ignore these calls. Because the Islamic understanding of intelligence includes action, a person who has emotional awareness and understanding yet doesn't follow that with action, is considered emotionally ignorant. A heart that is awake has a much greater responsibility than a heart that is asleep. It will not only notice pain in others, but those in pain will be able to notice this type of heart as well. While interpersonal emotional awareness is about learning how to see and listen with the eyes and ears of the heart, complete emotional intelligence also involves responding effectively to what the heart sees and hears. Many people choose not to engage in any type of emotional labor, as a defense mechanism for some and sheer laziness for others. Whether it be with their spouse, children, or parents, they choose to maintain relationships that are deprived of any deep emotional exchange. So many families are now lacking the most essential aspect of what it means to be a family. As an emotionally intelligent person, you will often have to do as the Prophet ﷺ did in this incident with the camel and become the means through which pain is communicated between two parties who are not able to understand one another. Although he owned the camel for quite some time, the camel's owner wasn't able to feel its pain. Why so? We all are blinded to the pains of those closest to us by the goals we set. A person with true emotional intelligence, not only masters interpersonal intelligence, but also masters intrapersonal intelligence; they can, in some sense, see themselves and their emotional and rational judgments objectively. In other words, they know themselves.

Perhaps the owner of the camel did not realize the pain and struggle the camel was experiencing, or felt justified and entitled in his actions by his struggle to provide for his family.

As the Prophet ﷺ walked away from the man, he ﷺ said, "Fear Allah regarding these animals that can't speak!" thereby obliging us to develop the ability to see with our hearts and make ourselves aware of the pain of those who can't articulate their feelings. This portion of the narration clearly places the burden of responsibility upon us to listen for the pain of those who can't express themselves. We should never become over-confident that the burdens we place on others are within their capacity simply because they don't say anything. Rather, we must "fear Allah regarding these *people* who can't speak" as well.

Another incident is equally revealing as the one previously mentioned. In the early years of the city of Madīnah, the Prophet ﷺ would deliver his Friday sermon leaning against a particular date-palm tree. As they became more settled in the city, some of the Companions offered a suggestion that a *minbar* be built for the Prophet ﷺ to stand upon when addressing the people. The Prophet ﷺ agreed, and the *minbar* was built. The day finally came for the Prophet ﷺ to begin using this *minbar*, so he ascended, then turned toward the people and began to speak. After a short time, the people in the *masjid* began to hear the sound of someone crying. The crying grew louder and louder, and the people could not figure out where the sound was coming from. The Prophet ﷺ then descended the *minbar* and approached the tree, who was now missing the Prophet's attention and companionship. He grabbed and hugged the tree close to his chest, and it began to calm down, trying to control its crying. The narration continues, explaining that the Prophet ﷺ then spoke to the tree, he asked if it would like to be moved close to the *minbar* and remain near him for the rest of his life or to be uprooted and buried and replanted in Paradise? The tree chose the latter and was uprooted and buried.

This incident is regarded as one of the most well-known miracles of the Prophet ﷺ. There were many Companions in the *masjid* and reports about this incident are abundant. But what was the actual miracle? What was so amazing about this incident? It is commonly explained that this incident is one of the great miracles of the Prophet ﷺ because a tree cried due to missing his company and trees normally don't talk or cry. However, from the lens of emotional intelligence, there seems to be another miracle that can be seen in this incident.

Abū Dharr relates that one day he went through the streets of Madīnah looking for the Prophet ﷺ. He suddenly found him sitting in one of the alleyways.

> So I approached the Prophet ﷺ and said to him, "*al-Salām ʿalaykum*." In front of the Prophet ﷺ on the ground were a few pebbles. He then grabbed the pebbles and they began to loudly glorify Allah while in his hand. He then placed them back on the ground, and they became silent again. Then he picked them up again and placed them in the hand of Abū Bakr who was also present and again the rocks began to loudly praise Allah. After a short time, he took them out of the hand of Abū Bakr and placed them back on the ground and again they fell silent. For a third time, he picked them up and this time placed them in the hand of ʿUmar ibn al-Khaṭṭāb. Again, the pebbles began to praise Allah. After taking them from the hand of ʿUmar and placing on the ground, he picked them up for a fourth and final time and placed them in the hand of ʿUthmān ibn ʿAffān, and they began to praise Allah again.

Again, the question is: what made this incident miraculous?

In my estimation, both narrations describe great miracles of the Prophet ﷺ, but the miracles lie not only in that fact that these things spoke, cried, or praised Allah. The miracle is not only the rocks loudly praising Allah, but rather that the Companions were granted temporary access to a level of awareness that the Prophet ﷺ regularly experienced. Similarly, the miracle when the tree cried is that the comprehensive interpersonal emotional awareness of the Prophet ﷺ was temporarily revealed to those present in the *masjid* that day. He constantly lived on a level of awareness that was far more perceptive than others. For him, it was normal. While for the companions and all others like ourselves, to live constantly in this highly perceptive state would make living a normal life almost impossible.

INCREASING INTERPERSONAL INTELLIGENCE

While some people seem to inherently possess a stronger sense of awareness than others, studies show that through training and focus, one can develop and increase their interpersonal intelligence. Intra- and interpersonal intelligence both require a high level of mindfulness. Many people struggle to notice the emotional states of others because they are not mentally present with them. Presence simply means that one's mind and heart are "with" the physical body and its actions. Ghazālī explains, "By mindfulness, we mean that the heart is free from any distractions and completely absorbed in whatever the person is doing or saying."[50] Others have defined mindfulness as "the capacity for sustained moment-to-moment awareness." The overlap of these two definitions is clear; however, from the prophetic perspective, mindfulness has a much deeper meaning. It is almost common knowledge that when a single action or set of actions is frequently repeated, our brains create neurological pathways to facilitate the repetition of those actions. Driving to work on the first day of the job may be tricky, but after making the trip every single day it becomes a "no-brainer"; you don't have to think to do it. This natural process allows us to focus on other things while we are doing those activities that we do every day. We become considerably more efficient due to the habitual nature of these actions. There is, however, a drawback to this. As actions become more automated, we no longer remain mindful of them. With the loss of mindfulness, there is also a loss in intent and deliberation.

50 Ghazālī, *Iḥyā' ʿUlūm al-Dīn*, vol. 1, p. 598.

When the Prophet ﷺ explained that all actions are judged by their intentions, he was teaching us that we should strive to remain cognizant of our deeper motivations and never slip into a state of mindlessness, or else life will begin to lose its deeper meaning and purpose. Let's look at prayer, for example. Muslims pray at least five times a day. Prayer is a foundational practice in Islam, and the Prophet ﷺ placed a lot of emphasis on the prayer being an integral part of a Muslim's life. The *salah* (ritual prayer) involves a set of physical movements along with verbal statements that accompany those movements. When converts first learn how to pray, there is a substantial amount of focus and concentration needed to perform *salah* correctly. But as this prayer is repeated day after day, the ease with which it is performed increases. Before you know it, a person may be able to perform the entire prayer without having actually thought about the actions they performed or the words they recited. The quality of the prayer is, however, based on one's ability to maintain mindfulness throughout it. Praying without focus is a topic that is discussed extensively and warned against in the Qur'ān, Hadith, and other Islamic literature.

Another major problem with lacking presence and mindfulness is that it communicates a lack of value for the person or action you are physically engaged with or in. The most valuable gift you can give a person is the one thing that you truly possess: yourself at the present moment. The most disrespectful message that we can communicate to people around us is that they are worthy of our physical presence but not our mental presence. Smartphones and other distractions have destroyed many families because we have lost the ability to prioritize where our mental presence should be. In one narration, the Prophet ﷺ describes that when a person gets distracted while praying, Allah calls out to the person saying, "Are you going somewhere better than me?"[51] According to Imam Mālik, if there is not at least one moment of mental presence with Allah during the performance of prayer, it is invalid. The

51 Mundhirī, *al-Targhīb wa al-Tarhīb*, vol. 1, p. 209.

presence of mind is a goal and objective of Islamic spirituality and it is the first step to building both intra- and interpersonal intelligence.

Paying close attention to those around you requires developing within yourself concern and empathy. There are very sound narrations in which the Prophet ﷺ strongly discouraged his companions from coming to the *masjid* after eating raw garlic or onions. The rationale behind this order shows his level of mindfulness for others; he explained that the Angels are disturbed by the smell of raw garlic and onions and that they are generally bothered by the same things that people are disturbed by. In this way, he effectively raised the standard of awareness to the realm of the unseen creation.

THE LANGUAGE OF EMOTION

Be it the crying of a tree or a camel; the Prophet ﷺ was able to both hear *and* listen with his heart. As the intellect is perfected, it will become aware of the slightest changes, as indicated in the well-known Arabic saying العاقل تكفيه الإشارة, "for the intelligent person a small gesture is sufficient." Some people seem to lack the emotional awareness necessary for positive interactions with others because they simply don't understand the language of emotions. Slight eye movements, body positioning, and verbal inflections are gestures that can communicate pain, anxiety, and joy. Unfortunately, many of us don't read these signs correctly. Looking back at the camel that began to grunt as the Prophet ﷺ approached, is it possible that this camel communicated to others, but they failed to understand? People are similar in that they will communicate the feelings of their heart through very subtle gestures and, if they see you are emotionally intelligent and receptive, they will begin to tell you their entire heart's story through the subtlest actions.

The one who understands the communicative functions of gestures becomes extremely conscious of the messages that their own body sends. Knowing the potential of body language, we see that the Prophet ﷺ possessed and taught something that Gardner calls "bodily intelligence." Wāthila ibn al-Khaṭṭāb tells us that, "A man once entered the *masjid* while the Prophet ﷺ was sitting down." It must be kept in mind that the *masjid* was relatively empty, but "as the man walked into the *masjid*, the Prophet ﷺ moved over" as if to make space for the man who just walked in. The man, noticing that his entry caused the Prophet ﷺ to move, said, "O Prophet of Allah, there is plenty of space in this *masjid*." Looking at the man, the Prophet ﷺ replied, "It is the right of a Muslim that when his brother sees him approach that the former at least makes some movement for him."[52] A person who possesses bodily intelligence understands the power of subtle gestures and the messages that are communicated through such slight movements. The messages communicated through such gestures may be remembered forever by the people we interact with.

Kaʿb ibn Mālik was boycotted for over 50 days by the Prophet ﷺ and the other companions when he was truthful about his failure to participate in the Battle of Tabūk. He said that he was sitting on his rooftop, having just completed his morning prayer, when he heard someone yelling from a distance, "Glad tidings, O Kaʿb! Glad tidings!" Understanding that this meant that the Prophet ﷺ must have informed the companions that the boycott was to be lifted, he ran to the *masjid*. On his way to the *masjid*, people were greeting him one after the other, congratulating him about his pardon. He says, "I entered the *masjid*, and the Prophet ﷺ was sitting down with a few people gathered around him. Ṭalḥa ibn ʿUbayd Allah stood up and ran toward me, congratulating me. No one else stood up." The emotional impact of Ṭalḥa's actions towards Kaʿb is clear from Kaʿb's next statement. He said, "And I will never ever forget Ṭalḥa due to his standing up for me." Many of us have experienced the power of slight movements and gestures as we enter a class, lecture, or gathering. We walk in looking for someone to acknowledge us and make some welcoming gesture. Perhaps they move a bag or a purse sending you a message that not only are you

52 Bayhaqī, *Shuʿab al-Īmān*, vol. 11 p. 273.

welcome but here is a place to sit if you like. Unfortunately, we have also been to those gatherings where, from the moment we walked into the room until we left, we felt as if no one even knew we were there.

BODY LANGUAGE

As mentioned above, one of the primary reasons we lack interpersonal emotional awareness is that we often don't understand, or we misunderstand, the language that emotion speaks. Love, pain, anger, and frustration are more often than not communicated through nonverbal cues. Albert Mehrabian explains in *Silent Messages* that nonverbal behavior is often more important than words when communicating feelings and attitudes towards others. When estimating the total feeling and emotions communicated by a person, he concluded that:

- 7% is verbal;
- 38% is vocal tone/expression; and
- 55% is facial expression.

The power of body language is learned early by youth growing up in rough neighborhoods. Navigating the inner cities of any American city forces them to learn how to walk and carry themselves in a way that doesn't invite trouble. Getting to school every day is dependent upon one's street smarts. The first lesson a young man or woman growing up in these places learns is that there are many ways to miscommunicate intent, and there's a complicated system of rules determining which emotion to show when. Let's take eye contact, for example. I cannot count the number of times I have de-escalated a situation just by using the right amount of eye contact. I can also remember one occasion where staring at a guy for 5 seconds too long led to an all-out brawl moments later. Though most of these skills are learned firsthand, a general rule of thumb is that complete avoidance of eye contact can cause would-be predators to view you as easy prey, while too much eye contact can equally invite trouble. The challenge of balance is to show strength and confidence through eye contact without antagonizing the other. I give these details only to show how and why encoding and decoding body language is such a delicate and difficult skill.

Equally challenging is learning how to modulate your gait. Encoding and decoding emotions through walking style is another skill that those who possess a sharp emotional awareness must learn to master. In almost every setting, your gait communicates an endless number of messages to those around you. Verses in the Qur'ān highlight the importance of learning how to walk and what messages should be communicated through your walking style. Describing the ideal qualities of His servants, Allah says,

> And the servants of the All-Merciful are they who walk on the earth gently and when addressed by the ignorant say, "Peace!"[53]

Similarly, in another verse, Allah commands, "Do not walk proudly on the earth."[54] The books of *shamā'il* offer quite a bit of detail regarding how the Prophet ﷺ himself walked; it is reported by many companions that when he walked, he would lean slightly forward. He also walked quickly and with intent and focus toward the direction he was going with very little looking around. Generally speaking, his gait communicated focus, intent, and humility at all times.

One of the clearest indications that he understood the importance of gait as a form of communication is found in a narration from the battlefield. It is narrated that Abū Dujāna was once walking extremely arrogantly in front of the enemy lines as the Prophet ﷺ arranged the soldiers for battle. Seeing the manner in which this Companion was displaying his strength and confidence, the Prophet ﷺ understood the situational benefit of his gait but wanted to warn his community at the same time. The Prophet ﷺ said, "This is a gait which Allah hates, except in this situation!" The way we walk tells the observant ones around us countless things about who we are and what is in our hearts.

53 Q 25:63.

54 Q 17:37.

PHYSICAL TOUCH

Lastly, I would like to point out how the Prophet ﷺ regularly used physical touch to communicate love and to comfort those who were in pain and suffering. Once, a man complained to the Prophet ﷺ that he suffered from hard-heartedness. The Prophet's ﷺ remedy for this spiritual sickness was for him to touch the head of an orphan. By this, he taught us that physical contact can be a healing for both the one being touched as well as the one touching. There are many other narrations that indicate that there is great power in touch. Our sensitivity to skin-to-skin contact is extremely powerful, and it has the power to heal when combined with a selfless, compassionate heart.

People with high levels of interpersonal intelligence understand, almost intuitively, the power and communicative capacity of physical contact and can easily communicate through these methods. A frustration voiced by multiple Muslim women we interviewed regarding their marital relationships was that their husbands seldom touched, held, or caressed them. These women justly felt that they were being emotionally neglected because their husbands failed to understand that a simple hug and kiss, with mindfulness and presence, can be an amazingly powerful emotional investment and means of providing comfort.

Our skin is our largest sensory organ. It is literally our contact with the outer world, and as Dr. Dacher Keltner of the University of California, Berkeley writes, "Touch is the first language we learn."[55] It is the first sense we acquire and the last that we lose. When current research regarding how touch communicates positive and negative messages is compared with the Prophet's use of touch to communicate with those around him, one can't help but appreciate the depth of his emotional understanding. We also see that the Prophet ﷺ used positive touch as a method of therapy and healing for those suffering from physical, emotional, or spiritual ailments. Discussing the power

55 Hertenstein & Keltner, 2006.

of a simple handshake, the Prophet ﷺ said, "Shake hands with one another because it removes malice from the hearts." Discussing the power and meaning behind shaking hands, Mehrabian writes, "Since a handshake involves bodily contact, it increases immediacy. Thus an individual's general level of preference for handshakes reflects how positively he feels toward others."[56] Qāḍī 'Iyāḍ narrates in his book, *al-Shifā'*, a statement of Anas ibn Mālik in which he describes the manner of the Prophet Muḥammad's ﷺ handshakes with other people: "Whenever a person would shake his hand, the Prophet ﷺ would not let go until the other person let go first. . .he was always the first to shake a person's hand." It was also common to see the Prophet ﷺ holding the hand of the person he was walking with. This extended platonic affection between two friends is common in many eastern cultures, while American and British friends touch each other far less during the course of a conversation. Alberto Gallace of the University of Milan-Bicocca writes in his report on *The Science of Interpersonal Touch*, "In the animal kingdom, touch is not only used for comfort but to establish bonds. . .Not surprisingly, therefore, touch seems to be even more important in those species that can be defined as social animals."[57] Extended handshakes increase what Mehrabian calls immediacy between two people: forming strong bonds and connection between them. We are wired to connect.

Reading the prophetic narration regarding the effect of a handshake, I can't help but remember my early days in Little League football. There were numerous lessons learned on those practice fields, many of which had more to do with becoming an honest young man than learning football. Football, of course, is a physical and competitive sport and with dozens of young men with elevated testosterone levels, all on one field, the occasional fight was a natural part of the season. Fighting destroyed team unity, so there was zero tolerance for it. The punishment for fighting was almost always the same: the two fight-

56 Mehrabian, *Silent Messages*, p. 7.

57 Gallace & Spence, 2008.

ers would be forced to run laps together until the coach felt they had learned their lesson. After that, the coach would look both young men in the eyes and give them some strong words of admonishment, and finalize everything by making them shake each other's hands. I always remember how hard it was to shake hands at the moment, but also how that one handshake genuinely cleared all the negativity between myself and the other person.

Lorraine Green of the University of Nottingham has written extensively on the power of human touch and its primacy in communication and development. In an article titled *The Trouble with Touch. New Insights and Observations on Touch for Social Work and Social Care,* she writes, "Touch is highly significant in our everyday encounters, relationships, and emotional, social, and even physical development."[58] David Linden, a neurobiologist at Johns Hopkins University, writes in his book *Touch, The Science of Hand, Heart and Mind*, "Touch is not optional for human development. . .we have the longest childhoods of any animal, and if our long childhoods are not filled with touch, particularly loving, interpersonal touch, the consequences are dramatic."[59] Because of an increase in sexual predators, our children often grow up in haphephobic environments. Looking back at the various narrations about how the Prophet ﷺ interacted with his young grandsons, frequently hugging and kissing them, we see how well he exemplifies Dr. Linden's point. Jābir ibn Samurah relates a story about a morning he spent with the Prophet ﷺ. He says,

> I prayed with the Messenger of Allah ﷺ the morning prayer. He then left the *masjid*, and I accompanied him. He was met by a group of children and rubbed their cheeks one by one. Then he rubbed my cheek, and his hand was cool and fragrant as if he had just taken it out of a perfume vendor's bag.[60]

---

58 L. Green, The trouble with Touch? New Insights and Observations on Touch for Social Work and Social Care. *The British Journal of Social Work*. 2017.

59 Linden, *Touch: The Science of the Hand, Heart, and Mind.*

60 Muslim, *Ṣaḥīḥ Muslim*, vol. 4, p. 1814.

This was not an isolated occurrence; in fact, it was a common practice of the Prophet ﷺ to pat children on the head, pray for them, joke with them, and sometimes wrap a turban around their heads.

As Sā'ib ibn Yazīd aged, his hair naturally began to grey and eventually turned white. However, there was a patch of hair on his head that remained its original vibrant color. He was asked by his servant, ʿAta, one day, why all his hair was white except for this patch. "Shall I tell you, my son?" "Indeed!" ʿAta replied. "I was once playing with other boys when the Messenger of Allah ﷺ passed by. I walked up to him and greeted him, he returned my greeting and then asked, 'Who are you?' I said, 'I am Sā'ib ibn Yazīd, son of al-Nimr ibn Qāsit's sister.' The Messenger of Allah passed his hand over my head saying, 'May Allah bless you!' By Allah! I don't think these hairs will ever go white and they will remain this way until I pass away!"

ʿAbd Allāh ibn Bishr was a young boy during the life of the Prophet ﷺ, and he was once sent by his mother to take a bunch of grapes to the Prophet ﷺ. He says, "Before reaching him I ate some of the grapes. When I arrived, the Prophet ﷺ passed his hand over my head. He then jokingly said to me 'Traitor!'" Later on, Ibn Bishr used to show them a mark on his forelocks, saying, "This is where the Messenger of Allah put his hand when he said, 'He will reach the century!'" Abū Zayd al-Ansāri was another young boy who was touched by the Prophet ﷺ. He relates that "The Messenger of Allah passed his hand over my head and while doing so he prayed for me saying, 'O Allah, make him beautiful and preserve his beauty!'" It is reported that Abū Zayd lived until he was well over a hundred years old without any grey hairs appearing in his beard and his face remained smooth until he passed away.

A husband who lacks interest in initiating skin-to-skin contact with his spouse can have a negative effect on his spouse's sense of satisfaction and fulfillment, as touch is a primary mode of communication. Even our emotional vocabulary is very touch-centric. "You're out of touch." "She's rough!" "His move was smooth"—these statements describing personality are based on our sense of feeling or touch. Can touch alone communicate emotions? Dr. Keltner and Matthew J. Hertenstein conducted a study[61] to test how well people were able to communicate emotional feelings to another person by simply touching the receiver's forearm. Students in an introductory psychology class at the University of California, Berkeley, ranging from 18 to 40 years, participated in this study. The 212 students were randomly assigned to one of two roles. The encoder's task was to communicate twelve emotions to the person sitting across from them: the decoder. The decoder's task was to interpret the emotion being communicated to them. Decoders were asked to sit on the opposite side of a black curtain and put their arm underneath to the side of the encoder. The decoders could neither see their own arm nor the person touching their arm. Twelve cards were then shown to the encoder, one at a time. The encoder was told to communicate each emotion to the other person by simply touching their arm, in any way that they felt would best communicate the emotion listed on the card. The decoder was given a questionnaire with all twelve emotions listed and asked to choose which emotion was being communicated to them. The results showed that decoders had a 48%–83% accuracy. Dr. Keltner's conclusion was that humans can communicate several distinct emotions through touch, but we don't completely understand how touch communicates.

Mehrabian, the author of *Silent Messages*, was a pioneer in the field of nonverbal communication. He felt that touch played a very important role in human communication and that it ultimately determined the total impact of the message regardless of the clarity of other verbal or nonverbal cues. Accordingly, he wrote, "touching, positions (distance, forward lean, or eye contact), postures, gestures, as well as facial and vocal expressions, can all outweigh words and determine the feeling conveyed by a message."[62] Many narrations describe how often the Prophet ﷺ initiated physical contact with his wives. ʿĀ'isha

61 Hertenstein, Keltner, *Touch Communicates Distinct Emotion*, 2005.

62 Mehrabian, *Silent Messages*, p. 45.

narrated that, "Whenever the Messenger of Allah had concluded the ʿAsr prayer (late noon) he would enter the house of [one of his wives] and would become intimate with her." A similar message is found in another narration where she says, "It was rare that the Prophet ﷺ of Allah would not visit all of us. He would *socialize* with one of us, without reaching intercourse. He would go around until he reached the house of the one whose turn it was that day and spend the night at her house."[63] In explaining this narration, the well-known commentator ʿAynī said that ʿĀ'isha's statement meant that he would physically touch her and fondle her without reaching the point of sexual intercourse. This narration shows the affection and interpersonal physical attention that he would show to his wives. It seems quite interesting that ʿĀ'isha went out of her way to mention that his physical touch was not intended to lead to intercourse, indicating that he understood that his wives had an emotional need to be touched and held. Dr. Tiffany Field, of the Touch Research Institute, explains how a massage from a loved one can not only ease pain but also soothe depression.[64] This perhaps explains the reason why the Prophet ﷺ touched the camel that was complaining and the tree that was crying due to its separation from him. A warm touch sets off a release of oxytocin, a hormone that helps create a sensation of trust and reduces levels of the stress hormone, cortisol.

In his commentary on the ḥadīth collection of Bukhārī, Ibn Ḥajr points out that the Prophet ﷺ would meet his wives twice a day, once in the morning and once in the evening. In the morning, the Prophet ﷺ would simply meet them to talk to them and pray for them. In the evening the Prophet ﷺ would spend more time sitting with them, getting close to them, and having long talks with them.[65]

This sensation of trust was often described as a direct result of the Prophet's touch as well. Ibn Hisham narrates an interesting account

63 Abū Dawūd, *Sunan Abī Dawūd*, vol. 3, p. 470.
64 Tiffany Field, *Touch*, p. 40.
65 Ibn Ḥajr, *Fatḥ al-Bārī*, vol. 9, p. 379.

regarding a Companion of the Prophet ﷺ named Fuḍālah. Although the Muslims were victorious after the conquest of Makkah, there were many people who maintained extreme animosity for the Prophet ﷺ and Islam. Immediately after the conquest, the Prophet ﷺ was circumambulating the Kaʿba when Fuḍālah ibn ʿUmayr, who was not Muslim at the time, thought to himself that he should take this opportunity to kill him. He drew near as the Prophet ﷺ was going around the Kaʿba, and as he came close, the Prophet ﷺ turned and looked at him and called his name, "Fuḍālah?" as if to confirm he was speaking to the right person. "Yes! Fuḍālah, O Messenger of Allah!" he replied. "What were you just thinking to yourself right now?" "Oh, nothing at all! I was simply praising Allah!" he replied in a state of shock. The Prophet ﷺ laughed, and as he turned his head away from Fuḍālah, he said to him, "You should seek Allah's forgiveness!" clearly referring to Fuḍālah's intention to kill him. The Prophet ﷺ then turned and placed his hand on the chest of Fuḍālah, and a sudden peace flowed through his heart. Fuḍālah, when relating this incident, would say, "I swear by Allah! By the time he took his hand off my chest, none of Allah's creation was dearer to me than him!" That single touch from the beloved Prophet ﷺ created such a deep change within Fuḍālah, a man who was thinking just moments before that he should assassinate the Prophet, that he was transformed in an instant. We have to learn how to touch those in need similarly to the way the Prophet ﷺ touched people. Fuḍālah's heart was filled with rage and anger, and it knew no other recourse to alleviating that rage than through bloodshed. It was a touch of peace and love that removed those noxious emotions from his heart. Albert Gallace says, "interpersonal touch appears to be capable of modulating people's compliance. . .we simply can't understand touch."[66] Immediately after this incident, Fuḍālah passed by the house of a woman with whom he used to sit and flirt. As he passed, she noticed him and called him over. His reply to her from a

66 Gallace & Spence. The Science of Interpersonal Touch: An Overview. *Neuroscience and Biobehavioral Reviews*. 2008.

distance was, "No, Allah will not allow it, nor Islam!" He then recited an impromptu poem about the beauty of Islam and the Prophet ﷺ.

EMOTIONAL UNDERSTANDING

A traditional fable tells of a village terrified by the presence of an angry lion that prowled around the village, taking away any feeling of security from the villagers. Terrified, the town's people agreed to kill the lion to bring back peace and security to their village. Androcles was a young slave who worked as a shepherd for his cruel master. Completely disgusted with his lot, one night he made up his mind to run away from this miserable life. Upon doing so, he found himself caught in a terrible rainstorm and decided to spend his first night of freedom in an unoccupied cave safe from his master and the terrible weather. As he made himself comfortable in the cave, his feelings of security abruptly ended as he realized that the cave he chose was occupied by the angry and hungry lion that terrorized his town. Realizing he was about to be ripped to shreds, he accepted his fate and prepared himself for the attack. As the lion approached, however, he noticed that the angry roaring of the lion was not due to his insatiable appetite, but rather due to a thorn stuck in its paw. Taking the risk, he approached the lion, and delicately removed the thorn. The lion immediately became calm and started gently licking the young shepherd as a sign of his love and appreciation.

Emotional understanding of others will give us deeper insight into why the ones we love are acting and feeling the way they are. The lion in this fable knew the source of his pain was but was unable to communicate his need for help. In this type of situation, an emotionally intelligent person has first to identify, then delicately remove the psychological or emotional thorn. As self-ignorance increases in our societies, chances are that the lion that you are dealing with will not understand why it is acting the way it is. If you wish to navigate your relationships with other people in a prophetic manner, you will have to learn why people feel and act the way they do. This comprehension is based on your ability to understand yourself. If you cannot understand why you feel what you feel and why you act the way you do, you will never be able to identify and understand the feelings of others.

The capacity to identify the sources of suffering in other people is thus the third pillar of emotional intelligence, and it plays a pivotal role in family, communal, and societal reform, as people are becoming increasingly disconnected. The emotionally intelligent person looks for the sources of pain and suffering of the people around them and understands that emotional outbursts are, at their essence, pleas for help. The emotionally intelligent Muslim takes lessons from the life of the Prophet Muḥammad ﷺ and works to develop this understanding within themselves because, without it, they cannot fulfill their duty to emulate the Prophet ﷺ.

In the previous section, we discussed intrapersonal and interpersonal intelligences as they relate to emotional awareness. It should be noted that the early stages of development of these intelligences fall under the broader category of emotional awareness. However, as they are developed and sharpened, they eventually grow from a simple awareness to a deeper understanding. An emotionally unaware person fails to register their own or others' feelings, and simply doesn't notice the changes in others' behavior, let alone understand the emotions behind those changes. The person who has developed both intelligences is not only aware of but also understands what is taking place inside themselves and other people. Emotional awareness is simply one's ability to see or perceive emotional shifts, whereas emotional understanding is one's ability to understand the forces behind those shifts.

Imagine that your car won't start or it starts making a weird noise. We may open the hood and stare at the engine, often having no clue about the cause of the problem. It seems that simply looking at the engine and even touching a few things here and there gives us a sense of having tried to do something. We are aware of a problem, but we lack a deeper understanding of the problem. Similar is the case with the emotional changes that take place within our own hearts and minds or within those of others. The mechanic, on the other hand, can often understand the problem and solution just by asking the person a series of questions. If the car is not starting, they know immediately where to begin. The difficulty, however, is that each manufacturer designs cars differently. The expert BMW mechanic may not be as skilled at understanding the problems in a Cadillac. Of course, human beings are infinitely more nuanced than cars, but this example gives the reader insight into the kind of personal intelligence they need to develop in their own lives.

This example also sheds light on one more aspect of emotional intelligence which we hinted at in the last section. That is, emotional awareness and emotional understanding do not necessarily lead a person to choose to use that knowledge for the betterment of themselves or other people—just as some car mechanics use their knowledge to rip off those who are ignorant. Many people use their emotional understanding of people for their own selfish, worldly benefit. This is where one's moral intelligence must come into play. The Prophet ﷺ set the example before his followers of the complete *ʿaql*. Speaking quite frankly, Hell will be filled with many people who were extremely emotionally intelligent, who used that intelligence to con, scam, and mislead people. It is a tool that should be used for helping people and not an ultimate objective in and of itself. Many emotional abusers seem very observant and possess a deep understanding of those they abuse and manipulate. They know what buttons to push and precisely how hard to push those buttons. Without a well-developed moral intelligence, emotional understanding and awareness can be quite dangerous.

BEGIN WITH LISTENING

The Arabic saying, "The tongue is the interpreter of the heart" reminds us that we have become true listeners when we have mastered the ability to hear beyond the spoken words and listen to what the heart is saying. From this perspective, the Qur'ānic verse, "Only those who hear can respond,"[67] seems to remind us that we can only respond to what we listen attentively to. So, if we are deaf to the language of emotion, and if we don't understand the emotions behind nonverbal communication, we will never be able to respond appropriately.

Developing the ability to listen deeply can be difficult. The Prophet ﷺ used a method we now call *mirroring*. It is a method commonly used in marriage counseling and is extremely effective when used regularly. Mirroring is when the partner who is receiving a complaint or any other type of message from their spouse attempts to repeat the emotional message behind the verbal complaint back to their spouse. Of course, mirroring is not restricted to verbal communication. As we stated before, emotions are primarily communicated nonverbally. This means that learning how to apply the mirroring method to nonverbal communication is also a vital element of a strong emotional understanding. Mirroring, when implemented repeatedly, helps a person who is normally very reactionary build an empathic capacity to think more deeply about the person they are dealing with. Mirroring our partner's emotional pleas has a secondary benefit of allowing our partners the chance to think about what they themselves are actually feeling. They can learn more about themselves as they look in the mirror provided to them by their partner or friend. This helps them increase their own self-awareness and thus the emotional intelligence of the relationship increases. ʿĀ'isha narrated that the Messenger of Allah ﷺ left her room one night, "So I became jealous and acted differently toward him when he returned." Upon returning, the Messenger of Allah noticed the change in her demeanor, so he asked, "O, ʿĀ'isha, did you become

67 Q 6:36.

jealous?" She replied, "And why wouldn't someone like me be jealous over someone like you?" He replied, "I think your devil came to you" (suggesting the idea that he would go to someone else on her night).

Let us examine the incident more closely. First, we see the Prophet's ability to sense a change in ʿĀ'isha's emotions just through a shift in her body language. Secondly, we see his ability to identify and mirror the emotion behind the change. With clear, unambiguous language, he let her know that he knew what she was feeling. Many times, our loved ones do not want solutions to their emotional problems; rather, they desire someone who simply understands what they are feeling. All problems are not meant to be solved; some just need to be heard. Lastly, we see the Prophet ﷺ attempting to gently remove the source of her jealousy by explaining the source of this feeling. This prophetic method of understanding and responding to suspicion is in stark contrast to the messy situations that many couples find themselves in today. Inquiries about suspicious actions often play out like this.

Wife: "Where were you?"

Husband: "Why are you asking me where I was? You don't have the right to ask that."

Wife: "Are you hiding something?"

Husband: "Why don't you trust me?"

Notice here that the husband has failed to identify the real question and emotion underlying his wife's statement. His wife is really saying, "Why weren't you here for me?" This need for companionship and attention is what he should focus on first and foremost. Instead, he has defensively entrenched himself in a battle that can't be won. The wife, in the example above, has become emotionally *flooded*, a victim of emotional hijacking. Emotional flooding occurs when a person's emotional state takes control of them. The same way floodwaters take away everything in their path, similarly, people who are emotionally flooded cannot clearly hear the person with whom they are communicating; they subconsciously distort the messages they receive. At this point, his job is to soothe her distressed feelings by first recognizing the real issue and working to remove such thoughts. Such bouts of flooding are most often experienced as a result of very destructive and toxic self-talk. The Prophet ﷺ called this type of inner monologue the most deceptive form of inner speech.

Abū Zayd al-Balkhī (235 AH/849 CE), ninth-century physician and scholar of mental health, wrote extensively about destructive self-talk in his mental health manual, *Maṣāliḥ al-Abdān wa al-Anfus.* This book was first translated into English by Dr. Mālik Badri, one of the most renowned Muslim psychologists in the world today, as *Sustenance of the Soul.* His works discussing psychological matters within an Islamic paradigm have made him a pioneer of modern Islamic psychology.

It is quite interesting how he chose to translate the title of the book. The subject matter of the book is divided into two sections. The first section deals with maintaining bodily health, and the second section deals with psychosomatic disorders. Balkhī himself tells us that, to his knowledge, no one prior to him had written on the topic of mental health. In his introduction to the work, Dr. Faut Sezgin of the Institute of History of Arab-Islamic Sciences in Frankfurt, Germany, writes that Balkhī views the human composition as the combination of body and soul and that the health or sickness of either one of these two will have a direct effect on the other. The translator tells us in the introduction that, "He was also the first to classify emotional disorders in a strikingly modern way and to categorize them in one general classification. His nosology classifies neuroses into four types: Fear and panic; anger and aggression; sadness and depression; and obsessions." After listing the topics of each chapter, Dr. Badri conclusively states that Balkhī is a pioneer of psychosomatic medicine. We should also take into consideration how early Islamic physicians viewed mental health and its relation to the soul. Just as the Qur'ān explains that hearts can become sick, early 9th century Muslim physicians sought to classify mental illness and, thereafter, effectively treat it through cognitive therapy. Balkhī writes,

> We start by saying that since man is composed of a body and soul, he is bound to face from each part of them; fitness or weakness, health or sickness, or other symptoms that afflict his health in a negative way. The symptoms that afflict the body and upset its well-being are those such as fever, headaches, and various kinds of pains that affect the organs. The psychological symptoms that afflict a person are those such as anger, sorrow, fear, panic, and other similar manifestations.[68]

What is even more stunning than Balkhī's mental health analysis in the late 9th century is how long it took Western psychologists and physicians to develop a similar understanding. After explaining in vivid detail how the ideas of John Locke completely altered the English and French understanding of the relationship between the soul and mind, and consequently mental illness, George Makari writes, "and so as the 18th century commenced, the stage seemed to be set in England for mentalist views to sweep away the old and established themselves as the new paradigm for reason and its disorders."[69] One wonders how they failed to come in contact with the Islamic understanding of mental health that had been developed 800 years prior.

Returning to the discussion of the harms of persistent inner monologue, Balkhī advises those dealing with obsessive self-talk to quell such thinking by implementing what he calls external and internal methods. The external methods he suggests are preoccupation or keeping busy, and positive friends and well-wishers who can point out baseless, destructive self-talk. Someone sitting idly is more apt to fall into such thinking than a person who keeps their mind positively engaged in various activities. Keeping positive and compassionate company has clear merit within the prophetic tradition. Very often marital problems are amplified by the echo chambers of negative friendships. Instead of dismissing and refuting suspicious ideas, we

---

68 Badri, *Abū Zayd al-Balkhī's Sustenance of the Soul*, p. 26.

69 Makari, George, *Soul Machine; The invention of the Modern Mind*, p. 135.

find cases where friends fuel the flames of negativity and discord. Balkhī then explains the internal methods for dealing with obsessive self-talk and negative thinking,

> Internal thoughts are of two different types. The first is a collection of healthy thoughts that the person accumulates and stores in memory when in a healthy and relaxed state. They are retrieved from memory whenever the negative thoughts emerge.[70]

Resisting such inner speech means monitoring such thoughts, realizing that you don't have to believe them, and forcing oneself to bring to mind evidence to the contrary. It should be kept in mind that mirroring will be most effective overall when it is first practiced in less emotionally charged exchanges. Implementing these methods will increase the shared emotional intelligence of the relationship.

Inner thoughts and self-monologue prevent sustained presence; thus attunement is impossible, and rapport is lost. Let us look at another prophetic example that contains all of the key elements of interpersonal awareness.

While the Prophet ﷺ was sitting in the house of ʿĀ'isha, Zaynab bint Jaḥsh sent some food for the Prophet. As the servant entered and brought the food past ʿĀ'isha, she struck the hand of the servant causing the dish to fall to the ground and shatter into pieces. The Prophet ﷺ smiled as he bent down to collect the broken pieces, placing the food back in the dish as he pieced it together. "Your mother has become jealous," he said as he had a sound dish of ʿĀ'isha's brought and sent back to Zaynab. Notice his interpersonal understanding. He understood ʿĀ'isha's emotions well enough to know how to respond. He used comic relief to make those present feel comfortable in this awkward situation.

70 Badri, *Abū Zayd al-Balkhī's Sustenance of the Soul*, p. 63.

PARENTING PROPHETICALLY

"I am to you like a father, I teach you that which you are ignorant of," said the Prophet of Allah ﷺ to the group of companions gathered around him as he explained to them how to clean themselves after relieving themselves. The companions of the Prophet ﷺ were ridiculed for learning these seemingly trivial lessons, but the father of our community understood that it was his responsibility to teach us everything we would need to know in order to live a life pleasing to Allah. Recognizing their potential embarrassment in learning such a thing from him, he comforted them by saying, "I am like a father to you." Therefore, nothing was too insignificant for him to teach his followers.

Without developing the various capacities of emotional intelligence, it is nearly impossible for a person to live a life pleasing to Allah. Empathic understanding and compassion are the bases of prophetic guidance, human development, and human interaction. A plethora of recent studies now suggest that the foundation for emotional capacities like emotional management, emotional flexibility, and emotional understanding is laid primarily in early childhood.[71] An emotionally unintelligent adult is often the result and victim of emotionally unintelligent parenting methods. Children learn emotional management and understanding by imitating their parents' emotional reactions. With this truth established, this is why Allah had to bestow upon the Prophet ﷺ such a high level of emotional intelligence. As the father of our community, our level of emotional intelligence is directly correlated to his, inasmuch as we study and emulate him of course. What makes the Prophet's ﷺ intelligence even more interesting is that he was an orphan. His father died before he was born, and his mother died when he was only 6 years old. How could an orphaned child, who was unable to read and seldom traveled out of his birth town, obtain such

71 Ulutas, I., & Ömeroglu, E. (2007). "The Effects of an Emotional Intelligence Education Program on the Emotional Intelligence of Children." *Social Behavior and Personality: An International Journal*, 35(10), 1365.

a high level of emotional, moral, and social intelligence? Simply put, the Prophet ﷺ was taught by his Lord. The Prophet ﷺ had to model the highest level of emotional intelligence for his community because the community's subsequent collective level of emotional intelligence would only be as strong as the foundation established by his example.

Why is it that our children are drowning in anger, frustration, and insensitivity? Primarily, it is the result of emotionally inept parenting and the failure of parents to develop within their children cognitive flexibility, emotional understanding, and emotion management. Parental emotional intelligence research explains that common emotionally-inept parenting styles are associated with high levels of teenage insensitivity and harshness. More often than not, the insensitivity, harshness, and frustration we witness in children is simply the child imitating the emotional ignorance they witnessed in their parents. For example:

1. Ignoring feelings altogether—Such parents treat a child's emotions as trivial or a bother. They don't use the child's emotional changes as an opportunity to get closer to the child.
2. Being too laissez-faire—These parents notice how the child feels but believe that however a child handles the emotional storm is fine. These parents rarely step in to show their child an alternative emotional response. They will instead use bargains or bribes.
3. Being contemptuous and disrespectful—These parents show no respect for how the child feels. They are often harsh in both criticism and punishment.

If we believe that the foundations of emotional intelligence are laid in the first four years of a child's life, this means that every reaction, every frustrated outburst, and every moment of impatience is teaching the children around us how they too should handle emotional changes in the various situations they encounter. How parents react to frustrating circumstances, with or without emotional flexibility, is observed, learned, and imitated by their children. Older siblings will often scold or hit younger siblings when the latter frustrate the former, just as they themselves were scolded or hit.

Every morning before I head off to work, I make breakfast for my daughter, Mariyah, if she wakes up before I leave. Normally, the menu is one of three things: eggs, pancakes, or cereal. Now that she is six, she constantly wants to help as much as possible. That means cracking the eggs, mixing the eggs or the pancake batter and anything else that I let her make an attempt at. In the beginning, watching her do these things was unbearable. It was terribly messy and extremely slow. If I just did it myself, everything would be done so much quicker and definitely cleaner. What I learned from this daily morning ritual, however, was that my emotional presence with her while she tried her best to be a part of the process, was tremendously beneficial to her development and our relationship. It was my fault that I couldn't slow down enough to be with her while she learned. Even worse, she was also learning from me how to emotionally react to frustration and difficult situations. As she spills some of the eggs while stirring she looks up at me to see my reaction; this moment, I have come to learn, is the most crucial moment because it will be a real uncut version of how I react to small messes. It will be the very method she uses in the future to deal with the small messes that she will encounter later on in life or even later in the day with her little sister and brother. Daniel Goleman explains the importance of this type of interaction beautifully:

> Family life is the first place we learn emotional intelligence; in this intimate cauldron, we learn how to feel about ourselves and how others will react to our feelings; how to think about these feelings and what choices we have in reacting; how to read and express hope and fears. This emotional schooling operates not just through the things that parents say and do directly to children, *but also in the models they offer for handling* their own feelings and those that pass between husband and wife.[72]

72 Goleman, *Emotional intelligence*, p. 189 (emphasis mine).

Professor Albert Alegre conducted a study[73] in Northeast Spain and demonstrated how the time mothers spent in joint activities with their children correlated to their children's emotional intelligence. Letters were sent to over 750 families out of which 155 mothers and 159 children of these mothers participated. The study measured the following:

1. Mother-Children Time Spent Together
2. Emotional Intelligence
3. The Emotional Quotient Inventory
4. Trait Meta-Mood Scale
5. Single Emotional Intelligence Coefficient
6. Responsive Parenting

The mothers participating in the study were sent a questionnaire and a short time-log that they answered from their home. They were asked to fill out the time-log reporting how much time they spent with their children in joint activities and what those activities were. Their children were given a questionnaire at school assessing three of the six areas mentioned above.

The researchers concluded that their results were "consistent with previous research findings showing that parents' and children's' time spent together in joint activities relates to children's positive social and emotional outcomes and to adolescents' mental health." For some, this may seem like common sense, but what's even more interesting is that the study also tested the types of interactions that predicted the greatest positive outcomes. It was concluded that mother-child educational time together was the best predictor of children's interpersonal intelligence in comparison to time spent together watching TV or other activities that allow parents and children to be together, yet not interact. It was hypothesized that joint educational time was most influential because it requires parents and children to interact with one another in situations that are frustrating; to children, as they struggle

73 Alegre, 2012.

to learn new information; and to parents, as they attempt to teach new knowledge and skills. In simple terms, the most fruitful interactions for children's emotional intelligence growth are the most difficult ones. The study also showed that activities such as eating together, putting children to bed, and reminding children to clean were not predictors of children's emotional intelligence. Learning, struggling, and working together to solve a common problem is clearly an effective way for parents to increase their children's interpersonal skills.

Brother Muḥammad, a close friend of mine, once shared an enlightening experience that he had with his elderly grandfather. Muḥammad's grandparents were moving from one house to another, and he decided to live with them during the transition to make it easier for them. He explained to me that spending many hours interacting with his grandfather, day after day, taught him a lesson about the emotional support and presence that the elderly and young both need. Muḥammad explained,

> Throughout the day, my grandfather and I would do different things together. I would constantly attempt to do things for him, knowing that I could do them faster and more efficiently. When I would do this, my grandfather would clearly become frustrated with me. Then I slowly began to realize that what my grandfather wanted more than anything was for me to simply be there with him while he did things and not rush him through whatever it was he was trying to do.

Working with young children and the elderly is equally difficult for many of us for the same reason. We are so goal and outcome-oriented and constantly focused on finishing whatever it is that we are doing in the fastest time possible and doing it in the best way possible. The problem with this frame of mind is that it is completely contrary to how children learn. Children learn by doing. When you allow them to do something, they feel like they have a chance to show you how much they have grown. The goal and perfection-oriented mind feels that the outcome has more significance than the process; for the learning child, attempting the process in your presence with your emotional investment in their growth is the most fulfilling experience.

Anas ibn Mālik was a very young boy when he was sent to serve the Prophet ﷺ. He was like a son to the Prophet ﷺ and stayed close to him from the age of seven until fifteen or so. His narrations offer deep insight into how the Prophet ﷺ displayed emotional intelligence to the young people who were around him and interacted with him. Anas said, "I served the Prophet ﷺ for ten years, and I swear by Allah that he never said *uff*[74] to me even once. He never said about something I did, 'Why did you do that?' and he never said regarding something I didn't do, 'Why didn't you do such and such?'"[75] In a similar narration, Anas relates a specific incident that provides us with an excellent example of emotional education through emotional management. He says, "The Prophet of Allah ﷺ had the best character. One day he sent me to do something for him. I told him that I would not go play with the kids outside, but in my heart, I knew I wanted to play with the other kids. So, I left the house to do what the Prophet ﷺ asked me to do. But when I passed by other kids who were playing in the markets, I stopped and stood there with them. The next thing I noticed was the Prophet ﷺ standing behind me with his hand on the back of my neck. I looked back at him, and he was smiling. 'Hey Anas, did you go where I asked you to?' he asked me. 'Yes, I'm on my way right now!'"

Clearly, the Prophet's modeling of emotional flexibility and emotional management before this young boy had a deep impact on the heart of Anas. He learned how to respond when someone doesn't listen to you or when things aren't going as you expected them to. Anas tested the emotional and cognitive flexibility of the Prophet ﷺ and became a witness to its beauty as well. This positive learning experience can be understood through Anas' choice of words as he

74 Arabic expression of slight displeasure.

75 Muslim, *Ṣaḥīḥ Muslim*, vol. 4, p. 1805.

recalls this incident. He begins by saying, "The Prophet ﷺ had the best character!"

CORRECTING MISCONCEPTIONS OF FATHERHOOD

The Arab understanding of a father's role within the family made it more difficult for the Prophet ﷺ to teach his *ummah* the value and power of empathy and emotional understanding. The Arabs at the time of the Prophet ﷺ took pride in their ability to conceal their emotions as much as possible, which hindered their ability to accept Islam and follow his example because they couldn't understand the level of emotionality he displayed. Buraydah ibn al-Ḥusayb related that the Prophet of Allah ﷺ was giving a Friday sermon when suddenly Ḥasan and Ḥusayn, his two young grandchildren, came in wearing red garments, stumbling and falling over themselves. This beautiful sight touched the Prophet's heart so much that he descended from the pulpit and picked them up, then climbed the pulpit again and said to the congregation, "Allah has told the truth when He said, 'Your wealth and children are only a trial.' I saw these two and I was unable to have patience."[76] He then returned to his sermon. In front of this large congregation of men and women, the Prophet ﷺ showed his heart's compassion for his grandchildren and that these beautiful children were a source of weakness for him, in which he took pride. This small yet powerful act demonstrated that a man's love for his children and grandchildren is completely natural.

Another more explicit challenge of the Arabs' understanding of fatherhood is found in a narration by Abū Hurayrah where he said that the Prophet of Allah ﷺ once came out of his house carrying Ḥasan and Ḥusayn, one on each shoulder, and he was kissing each of them. When he reached the people, a man remarked to him, "O Messenger of Allah, you love them!" The Prophet ﷺ of Allah replied, "Whoever

76 Tirmidhī, *Sunan al-Tirmidhī*, vol. 5, p. 658.

loves them loves me, and whoever hates them hates me."[77] As we read through the various examples of the Prophet's interactions with his children and grandchildren, we must constantly remind ourselves that, though they may seem normal to us today, his actions were extremely strange in his culture. It was only natural that word of such public displays of affection spread to the neighboring areas of Madīnah. Thus, we find in a narration by ʿĀ'isha that a Bedouin came from outside of the city and upon meeting the Prophet ﷺ, he immediately asked, "Do you kiss your children? Because we don't kiss our children!" If we listen closely to the response of the Prophet ﷺ, we learn that he was attempting to completely reconstruct his people's understanding of masculinity. This reconstruction was necessary if he wished for his people to be the custodians of the prophetic inheritance and message. His response challenged the man's pride in his lack of affection. His reply, "What can I do if Allah has snatched mercy from your heart?"[78] was the powerful reply of a man fighting against a culture that took pride in heartlessness. Time after time, we see an unapologetic display of his loving nature. He was a man who understood his feelings and was not afraid to express them. The Prophet ﷺ experienced the deaths of all of his children except Fāṭimah. The reports of how he handled the deaths of his children and grandchildren also support the notion that his public display of emotion was constantly challenging the social norm and forcing his followers to truly embrace healthy emotional expression.

Anas ibn Mālik accompanied the Prophet ﷺ when his son Ibrāhīm passed away. He said, "I have not seen anyone more merciful with his family than the Prophet of Allah ﷺ. His son Ibrāhīm was being nursed outside of Madīna, and the Prophet ﷺ used to go and visit him. We too would accompany the Prophet ﷺ as he went. The husband of Ibrāhīm's wet-nurse was a blacksmith, so his house would often be filled with

77 Ibn Māja, *Sunan Ibn Māja*, vol. 1, p. 51.

78 Bukhārī, *al-Adab al-Mufrad*, vol. 1, p. 46.

smoke. I would often run ahead of the Prophet ﷺ and tell the husband that the Prophet ﷺ was coming so he could clear the smoke from the house and make it comfortable for him to visit his son. The Prophet ﷺ would come and take his son and kiss him and hug him. We came back another time and this time Ibrāhīm was breathing very heavily, the Prophet's eyes filled up with tears, and the tears began to run down the face of the Prophet. ʿAbd al-Raḥmān ibn ʿAwf looked up at the tears of the Prophet ﷺ and said, 'And you too cry, O Prophet of Allah?' The Prophet, with tears in his eyes, looked at ʿAbd al-Raḥmān and said, 'This is mercy,' and he continued to cry. 'Indeed, the eyes cry, and the heart hurts, but we will never say anything that displeases our Lord. O Ibrāhīm, we are deeply saddened by you leaving us.'"[79]

In a similar incident, Usāmah ibn Zayd was with a group of the Companions when one of the Prophet's daughters sent a message to him ﷺ urgently calling for him because her son was passing away. "The Prophet ﷺ stood up and with him was Saʿd ibn ʿUbādah, Muʿādh ibn Jabal, Ubay ibn Kaʿb, Zayd ibn Thābit, and a few other men." The Prophet ﷺ arrived at her house, "and the child was handed over to the Prophet, the child was having difficulty breathing and the Prophet's eyes filled with tears," Usāmah explained. "Saʿd then looked at the Prophet ﷺ and said, 'O Prophet of Allah, what is this?' referring to the tears filling up in the eyes of the Prophet. "These are signs of mercy," replied the Prophet ﷺ, "which Allah places in the hearts of His servants. Indeed, Allah will only have mercy on those who are merciful." Ibn ʿUmar narrated that the Prophet of Allah ﷺ said: "Ḥasan and Ḥusayn are my two flowers of this world."[80] Here, we see his ability to articulate his heart's feelings publicly. When a person has developed emotional awareness of themselves, it becomes much easier for them to communicate their feelings to the outside world. This type of communication serves two powerful roles. Firstly, as a Prophet ﷺ and an example to the people, it shows his community the importance of

79 Bukhārī, *Ṣaḥīḥ al-Bukhārī*, vol. 2, p. 83.

80 Tirmidhī, *Sunan al-Tirmidhī*, vol. 5, p. 655.

expressing feelings, and secondly, it communicates positive emotions to his grandchildren, thereby increasing their own emotional capacity.

As mentioned before, two of the key elements of emotional intelligence are emotional understanding and awareness. As parents, this means we must be completely cognizant of our children's feelings and how they will be affected by what we do, especially between the ages of one and four. One of the most powerful examples of the Prophet's awareness of his grandchildren's emotions is found a narration in the Hadith collection of Nasa'ī. He relates that "The Prophet of Allah came out for one of the evening prayers and he was carrying Ḥasan or Ḥusayn. He stepped forward, put him down, and then began the prayer. In the middle of the prayer, he made one of the prostrations very long. I raised myself from prostration and looked up and saw the child on the Prophet's back while he was prostrating, so I put my head back down. When the Prophet of Allah ﷺ finished the prayer, the people said, 'O Messenger of Allah, you made one of the prostrations long in the middle of the prayer, until we thought that something was wrong (like a sudden death or illness), or that revelation was coming down upon you.' The Prophet of Allah ﷺ said, 'None of that happened, rather my son rode on my back, so I did not want to make him move before he was finished.'"[81]

To completely grasp the overall level of empathy exhibited by the Prophet ﷺ in this narration, we must remember the seriousness of prayer for Muslims generally and for the Prophet ﷺ specifically. There are countless narrations that speak about the primacy of prayer for Muslims and, consequently, the importance of cultivating complete concentration and focus while praying. In one narration, the Prophet ﷺ said about prayer, "When a person prays they are standing before Allah." He also said, regarding his own connection with prayer, "The coolness of my eyes lies in prayer."[82] This is why the Companions who were praying behind the Prophet ﷺ thought that it had to be due to

81 Nasa'ī, *al-Sunan al-Sughrā*, vol. 2, p. 229.

82 Nasa'ī, al-*Sunan al-Sughrā*, vol. 7, p. 61.

something extremely serious, such as the death of the Prophet ﷺ or the descending of revelation. The justification for his extension shows that even while in the state of ultimate closeness with Allah, one must never become disconnected from the hearts of those around one.

I am probably not alone when I say that this narration has extra value for me as a father of three young children who are all under five years old. For them, every prostration is a chance to slide down my back or test their grip as they hang on for dear life to my neck when I stand back up from prostration. The prophetic example teaches a Muslim man how to combine his love and obedience to Allah with his love and emotional awareness of his children.

The Prophet's interaction with his youngest daughter, and only surviving child, Fāṭimah, shows his ability to use emotional intelligence to create a sense of self-worth, value, and love within others; this is what made him so beloved to her. A study of the Prophet's interaction with her supports Professor Alegre's theory that children learn most of their emotional intelligence from their parents. Fāṭimah's close relationship with her father seems to have provided her with a profound level of such intelligence. ʿĀ'isha, having watched the two interact extensively, says,

> I have never seen anyone closer in character and guidance to the Messenger of Allah ﷺ, in his looks, good conduct and in all of his affairs, more than Fāṭimah, the daughter of the Messenger of Allah ﷺ. When Fāṭimah, may Allah be pleased with her, visited the Prophet of Allah ﷺ, he would stand up to receive her, kiss her and seat her in his place. And when the Prophet of Allah ﷺ visited Fāṭimah, she would stand up to receive him, kiss him and seat him in her place.[83]

One can't help but imagine the level of honor she must have felt due to the respect that the Prophet ﷺ would show her. He stood up to receive

83 Abū Dawūd, *Sunan Abī Dawūd*, vol. 4, p. 355.

her, kissed her, and sat her in a place of respect, all in the presence of other people, further increasing her self-esteem and self-worth. His physical touch and kiss had a direct effect on her feelings. His welcome and love provided her with a feeling of comfort and security, not to mention the confidence that was built within her.

The studies mentioned above clearly inform us that parents play the most instrumental role in developing a child's emotional intelligence capacity. This also provides us with a deeper understanding of the prophetic model of sound parenting. A parent who fails to demonstrate strong emotional management before their children, has stunted their emotional growth, or worse, caused permanent damage to the development of this key aspect of the *ʿaql*. Every outburst of anger, every flustered moment, and every scream is registered as a potential method for dealing with emotions. Perhaps we could agree that children are a blank slate when it comes to dealing with emotions and it is we, their parents and caretakers, who write on that slate with our own actions and reactions.

III
Moral Intelligence

Up until now, we have simply presented the aspect of the *ʿaql* which attempts to discover how to effectively pass on the message of revelation to the rest of creation. Within the prophetic model of intellect, emotional intelligence is only praiseworthy because it allows one to effectively communicate the message of revelation to others and facilitates one's ability to fulfill the rights of the creation of Allah. An easy way to understand the ultimate function of emotional intelligence within our model is to revisit the word "messenger." At the beginning of the section on emotional intelligence, we stressed the importance of studying the messenger himself because he was divinely inspired with an unmatched emotional and psychological knowledge of people—a knowledge that facilitated the transfer of his message to those whom he called. For now, I will ask readers to focus on the message of the messenger rather than the messenger himself. Moral intelligence is the second half of the prophetic model of intelligence and the essential knowledge that was placed in the hearts of prophets to guide mankind on their journey back to Allah. Moral intelligence is defined by contemporary scholars as: "The capacity to process moral information and to manage the self in a way that realizes that moral ideal."[84]

84 Tanner, Carmen & Christen, Markus. (2013). Moral intelligence—A Framework

When Abū Ḥanīfa was asked, "What is true understanding?" he replied, "Knowledge of that which benefits the soul and that which harms it."[85] This definition, however, does not fulfill all the criteria necessary for complete moral intelligence. For this, we will have to turn to the Qur'ān.

There is one verse in the Qur'ān that brings together all five of the aspects of moral intelligence that will be discussed. This verse praises three prophets of Allah by highlighting two defining qualities that they possessed:

> And make mention of Our slaves Abraham, Isaac, and Jacob: men of power and insight.[86]

The function of moral intelligence is found in the words "power" and "insight." The first responsibility of the intellect is to "see" correctly. This means that a Morally Intelligent person can distinguish the morally upright from the immoral. Thereafter, a Morally Intelligent person can use their *ʿaql* to reach their moral ideal, and this is the power of the *ʿaql*. Discussing this verse, Ibn al-Qayyim explains the following,

> Human perfection rotates around two primary capacities: Knowing the truth from falsehood and giving preference to the truth. . .these are the two capacities that Allah praised in the verse, "And remember our slaves Abraham, Isaac, and Jacob those of power and insight." The word "hands" means the power to make the truth a reality, and the word "eyes" refers to religious insight. Thus they are described with perfection because of their ability to know the truth and their ability to make the truth come out.[87]

The moral education that the Prophet ﷺ provided his community

---

for Understanding Moral Competences, p. 1.

85 Mangera, *Imām Abū Ḥanīfa's Al-Fiqh al-Akbar Explained*, p. 65.

86 Q 38:45.

87 Ibn al-Qayyim, *al-Jawāb al-Kāfī*, Dār ʿĀlām al-Fawā'id.

worked to perfect the sight of the *ʿaql* and its ability. Towards the end of this section, we will provide a framework that breaks down moral intelligence into five specific areas. Collectively nurturing all five of these areas is the means towards developing a high level of moral intelligence.

SUBJECTIVE MORALITY

As a young boy in grade school, it was a daily ritual of mine to quickly finish my homework as soon as I arrived home and join the other neighborhood children for our pick-up football games. Looking back at these football games, I now realize that some of life's greatest lessons took place right on that small plot of grass across the street from my house. Looking back, I also realize that the children naturally understand the absurdity of subjective morality.

Before every game, both teams would meet in the middle of the field. The captains spoke while the others sized up their opponents. Occasionally, a bit of trash-talking would also take place. But another very important thing took place at this point. The rules of the game were settled and agreed upon and every street played by its own rules. Even at that young age, all the children on the field understood that if the rules were not set, a meaningful game was impossible, and it would be impossible to define a winner. These young children, preparing for their pick-up football game, understood the absurdity of subjective morality, or enforcing rules subject to the opinion of each player. For example, before the game even started, the "out-of-bounds" had to be established. Of course, this agreement did not stop the ensuing arguments regarding whether a catch was made in or out of bounds, but at least from the very beginning, it was agreed that such and such was the boundary. Once the game began, there would be no changing the rules.

The second half of the definition of moral intelligence revolves around the individual or collective ability to actually realize the moral ideals one has adopted; this necessitates that a person possesses a sound justification for their subscription to those moral ideals. Islamic moral education that produces sound justification of Islamic ideals serves two important purposes. First, and perhaps most importantly, sound justification is a necessary component of rational moral subscription. When moral subscription is irrational, the behavioral result is mere conformation, whereas rational moral subscription creates transformation. The need for sound justification of moral subscription is based on the context within which one finds oneself.

Insulated institutions that protect members from foreign influences may not see an immediate need for justified subscription. Educators in these environments are often satisfied when people simply comply. When a particular group finds itself to be a moral minority, the need for moral identity is increased. Here I mention moral identity because the strength of a justified subscription to a moral code and one's sense of their own moral identity are directly correlated.

For the Muslim, developing moral intelligence begins with an understanding of what the *ʿaql* does— it "sees" and it is that which "holds one back." In other words, it has the capacity to know and the capacity to control. In fact, knowledge is not considered praiseworthy from the prophetic perspective until it gains the title of *ʿilm nāfiʿ*, or beneficial knowledge, which is knowledge that produces positive change within a person. The word *Muslim,* or "one who submits," contains within it both aspects of the moral intelligence. The first is the submission to a moral standard that comes from other than oneself, and the second is the submission of the *nafs* to the *ʿaql's* demands upon it.

Weak and unstructured moral education programs have dealt a deadly blow to our collective moral intelligence. An equally concerning threat to our collective moral intelligence is explained by Peter Kreeft in *Ecumenical Jihad,*

> Unless two principles are as certain in our minds as they are in fact, we will continue to treat this cancer with aspirin and our society

> will die. . .First principle: the foundation of social order is morality. Second principle: the foundation of Morality is religion.[88]

MORAL INTELLIGENCE: A COMBINATION OF VISION AND STRENGTH

> And make mention of Our slaves Abraham, Isaac, and Jacob; men of power and vision.[89]

The second half of moral intelligence has to do with moral practice, while the first half revolves around one's ability to recognize moral truths. Subjective morality is particularly dangerous because it attacks the ʿ*aql's* sight. It effectively eliminates all debate surrounding good and evil by deeming the two as a matter of perspective. Once the ʿ*aql* believes that there are many non-competing truths, it no longer wishes to strive for ultimate good. There is no ultimate good. For this reason, C.S. Lewis said, "relativism is going to end our species and damn our souls." Moral relativism eliminates the law and therefore, also eliminates sin, repentance, and salvation. This is how it damns our souls. It claims that good and evil are man-made; they are merely based on one's perspective. The attempt to create a purely rational, secular morality is considered to be the major failure of the Enlightenment. As Dostoyevsky said, "If there is no God, everything is permissible."

The Islamic understanding of the ʿ*aql* in relation to Allah's command is profound in that the authority of conscience depends on the Authority of Allah. As we lean towards a subjective understanding of morality, moral practice becomes increasingly loose and weak. As Peter Kreeft puts it, "Subjective Morality is an oxymoron; it is not morality at all. . .If we make the rules, we can change them. If I tie myself up, I am not really bound." In other words, morality is something that binds you and keeps you from harming yourself primarily because it

88 Kreeft, *Ecumenical Jihad*, p. 17.

89 Q 38:45.

exists independent of you. Subjective morality is not morality at all. It's a goalpost that moves to wherever the kicker kicks the ball.

Peter Kreeft depicts the futile nature of subjective morality through the biblical story of the tower of Babel in Genesis 10. The story tells us that mankind, forgetting their dependence upon God, began to see themselves as unstoppable. They felt that nothing was beyond their grasp so long as they worked together. It was will-power and technology combined that made all things possible according to them. So they decided that they wanted to build a tower to the heavens and see their Creator. And so the construction commenced. As all mankind collectively strove to reach God, their tower grew higher and higher day by day until one morning God punished them by making their speech unintelligible to one another. They were all speaking different languages. No longer able to work together, the people dispersed throughout the earth, eternally divided by the barriers of language. This was a punishment for their audacity. It is from this story we get the English word "babbling" for unintelligible speech. They attempted to reach God through earthly means but failed.

It is only through God sending down revelation that mankind is able to connect to God. Revelation is the bridge by which man reaches God. It is a tower or bridge which descends to man. The two towers are drastically different. The tower of Babel has a limited, earthly foundation, so it lacks the strength to carry man to God, whereas revelation's foundation is in the heavens, which makes it strong enough for man to traverse. Similar is the case with subjective or relative morality: its foundation is here on earth so it can never bring man to his salvation.

A prophetically trained intelligence stands in stark contrast to the "therapeutic culture" of today. In *The Triumph of the Therapeutic*, Philip Rieff highlights the inevitable social collapse of America and the creation of a "therapeutic culture," which replaces theology with sociology. In his work *Deathworks,* he breaks down Western culture into three historic periods. The first being the pagan era, in which people had many deities, the second the age of monotheism, and the third (current age) era in which man attempts to do away with God altogether and thus destroy sacred order. In the third age, man defines himself by his attempt to sever all connection with God and, according to Rieff, the result is nihilism. He explains in *Deathworks* that "where there is nothing sacred, there is nothing." Not only does man in this third era wish to sever all connection to the sacred but he also attempts to destroy truth, and in so doing, he gives power to another god, the god of desire. Emotivism, which was discussed by MacIntyre in *After Virtue*, is the ethics of subjective, feelings-based personal preferences, which intends to quiet and calm social conflict but, in fact, only creates and exacerbates unresolvable disagreements. "Live and let live" becomes the de facto mantra of our modern culture. In the absence of a shared framework and agreed-upon values and virtues, moral disagreements are translated into political issues. Everything necessarily becomes political because, without a shared framework, rational discourse cannot take place. Self-determined and immune to critique, the individual's personal opinion regarding not only happiness, but how to achieve that happiness, has been given ultimate protection. In the emotivist culture, which goes hand in hand with liberalism, the highest political virtue becomes the maximization of individual choice. This, in turn, breeds a society in which the highest social virtue is tolerance. Brad Gregory argues in *The Unintended Reformation*, "A transformation from a substantive morality of the good to a formal morality of rights constitutes the central change of Western ethics in terms of theory, practice, and institutions."[90] The reality of private and public life that is often overlooked is that they are inseparable. In *Disenchantment*, Steven Smith explains that "what we do in private will almost certainly have a gradual and subtle, but very real influence on the sort of community all of us experience."[91] It comes back to the false assumption underlying the saying, "Do whatever makes you happy, so long as you're not hurting anyone else." We assume what counts

90 *The Unintended Reformation, Brad Gregory*, p. 184.

91 Smith, *The Disenchantment of Secular Discourse*, p. 86.

as "hurtful" is self-evident and agreed upon but, from a subjective or relative moral framework, almost nothing is agreed upon.

Early moral theorists who shaped this liberal framework were successful in convincing us that the moral views that people hold, and are free to hold, are subordinate to the foundational ethical imperative for individual liberty, and that politics and laws must be arranged according to that hierarchy. Simply put, the liberal framework places the pursuit of happiness above the pursuit of truth. This was done because it is assumed that this is the only way for people with drastically diverse understandings of the world to coexist peacefully. As John Stuart Mill expressed in *On Liberty*, moral pluralism is an unavoidable political challenge to be managed. "The only freedom which deserves the name freedom is pursuing our own good in our own way." What was considered "good" no longer mattered as personal feelings were sanctified, but the bitter and unexpected consequence of such an understanding was that as political rights were extended further and further, individuals were increasingly forced to tolerate the intolerable, inevitably resulting in friction and anger.

Perhaps what is more dangerous is when entire communities lose any sense of true unity and a basis upon which to promote a common good. Within the Islamic context, the Qur'ānic emphasis on good counsel loses all meaning because there is no common good. Each member of this emotivist society sees others only as a means to their own happiness. They all give up on persuading others. Each person is a standard of perfection for themselves and their own goals are the only ends because there are no ultimate ends outside of the person. The Muslim community's moral framework doesn't place virtue on this type of tolerance for two reasons. Firstly, because of its eventual destructive nature to the individual and community and secondly, because opinions warrant justification outside of the individual. The intellect demands consistency so that which is good for the individual should also be good collectively, without which the sense of community is slowly broken down. Extremely pluralistic societies, which have no shared framework, lack the most essential element of communal life: interpersonal trust. When a community collectively subjectifies truth, the most that one can expect, or demand is that others stay true to their individual framework of right and wrong. There simply is no shared framework to bond the individuals of the community.

ʿAQL'S SIGHT

Studying the early Islamic works on the *ʿaql,* one can't help but observe what I would consider somewhat of an intellectual fixation with understanding the nature and role of the intellect. Extensive works written on the concept of the *ʿaql* are found in every Islamic discourse; from theology to jurisprudence to spirituality, every science touches upon the reality, role, or function of the intellect. Upon closer investigation, it becomes clear that this scholastic obsession with the *ʿaql* simply echoes the Qur'ān's numerous logical arguments and pleas to humanity to simply use the gift of reason, open the eyes of the intellect, and conclude that sincere submission to Allah is what is best for them. In the Qur'ān, Allah repeatedly suggests that it is by means of this gift (i.e., the *ʿaql*) that humanity will all arrive in the presence of Allah. The *ʿaql* is the means by which humanity comes to know Allah and to know what He loves. It is also the ideal tool that should guide and determine people's actions. When strong, it will also compel people to act according to its moral subscriptions. Lastly, it will attempt to solve our individual and social problems without ignoring or sacrificing the divine code it was given. The *ʿaql,* the noun form of which is never used in the Qur'ān, is given various names like *nuhā'* (that which prevents) or *lubb* (the core or essence of something) to provide readers with deeper insight into its role and reality. From the Qur'ānic perspective, it is the intellect that seems to be exclusively admonished for disbelief, immorality, and social discord. Take, for example, the following verse of the Qur'ān wherein the heart, considered to be the seat of the *ʿaql,* is harshly criticized. But what exactly is the heart being criticized for?

> Have they not traveled in the land, and have they hearts to comprehend with, or ears to hear with? For it is not the eyes that become blind, but it is the hearts in the chest that have become blind.[92]

The verse uses the construct *yaʿqilūna bihā* ("think with it"), informing us that, from the Qur'ānic perspective, it is the heart that possesses the ability to think and contemplate and it is the heart that bears responsibility. A failure to think about, contemplate over, and witness Allah's creation and His signs therein is deemed the ultimate blindness of the heart. The "sight" of the heart or *ʿaql* is oft-repeated throughout the Qur'ān. For example, in verse 11 of Sūrah al-Najam, Allah describes the celestial night journey made by the Prophet Muḥammad ﷺ to His presence saying, "His heart did not lie about what it saw." Sight in this context must be understood as any mode or method of cognitive apprehension, such as our use of the phrase, "I see." But the scholastic tradition extends the role of the *ʿaql* beyond apprehension and cognition and includes moral subscription, moral commitment, and behavior modification. If we look at another verse that uses the word *yaʿqilūna,* we see an interesting pattern. In verse 164 of Sūrat al-Baqarah, Allah says,

> . . .In the creation of the heavens and the earth; in the alternation of night and day; in the sailing of the ships through the ocean for the benefit of mankind; in the water which Allah sends down from the sky and with which He revives the earth after its death; in the animals of all kinds He has scattered therein; in the ordering of the winds and clouds that are driven between heaven and earth, are signs for people who can think.[93]

In both verses, we see that Allah directs the intellect to look at the world and, by means of its sight (i.e., cognitive apprehension), develop a cognitive recognition of the greatness of the Creator. Recognition of Allah

92 Q 22:46.
93 Q 2:164.

is not the product of irrational moral subscription or indoctrination. Rather, true recognition of Allah is a type of knowledge that has the highest epistemological value: experiential. The emphasis placed on the intellect in these and many other verses, coupled with numerous prophetic narrations,[94] obliged Muslim scholars to discuss, in depth, the nature and role of the intellect.

Scholars of Islamic jurisprudence reduced all legal rulings back to five ultimate objectives, with the preservation of *ʿaql* being one of them. Ṣadr al-Sharīʿah al-Maḥbūbī (d. 747 AH/1347 CE), the author of several influential works on *uṣūl al-fiqh*, speaks about the pivotal position of the *ʿaql* in his work, *Tanqīḥ*, a commentary upon another of his works, *Tawḍīḥ*. In the section titled *'Those upon whom rulings are applied,'* he begins with the first and primary basis for legal responsibility. "It is necessary for a person to be suitable for a ruling. This will not be established except through one possessing intellect. . .it (the *ʿaql*) is the axis around which legal responsibility rotates."[95] Saʿd al-Dīn al-Taftāzānī further confirms the primacy of the *ʿaql*; commenting on this final point, he explains that it is through this faculty that "humans move from simple understandings to conceptual understandings and are thus differentiated from the beast."[96]

GOOD AND EVIL AND THEIR RELATION TO THE ʿ*AQL*

This brings us to a very important question: from the Islamic perspective, what is the relationship between good, evil, and the intellect? The discussion of good and evil is primarily found in two types of classical literature: jurisprudence and theology. From the perspective that good and evil are ultimately related to the commands and prohibitions of Allah, a person can easily come across this discussion in the books of

94 Prophetic narrations regarding the *ʿaql* are heavily debated within the field of Hadith qualification and authentication.

95 Maḥbūbī, *Tanqīḥ*, p. 327.

96 Taftāzānī, *Sharḥ al-Talwīḥ*, vol. 2, p. 315.

Usūl al-fiqh. But when observed from the perspective of the nature of good, evil, and the intellect, books on the subject of *Kalām*, or theology, are also a primary source for understanding this topic.

Al-Taftāzānī (792 AH/1390 CE), an early classical scholar in various fields but perhaps most renowned for his works in *Usūl al-fiqh* and *Kalām*, explains in his work, *Talwīḥ*[97] (which is his commentary on *Tanqīḥ*) that the terms *ḥusn* and *qubḥ* are used in one of three ways. Literally speaking, *ḥusn* (good) means beautiful, and *qubḥ* (evil) means ugly. The first is when someone says, "Sweet foods are *ḥusn* and bitter things are *qubḥ*." The second is when someone says, "Knowledge is *ḥusn,* and ignorance is *qubḥ*." The last of the three is what is debated within the framework of Islamic theological discourse; it is when someone says, "Such and such act of obedience is *ḥusn* or such and such act of disobedience is *qubḥ*." Al-Taftāzānī explains that all of the debates between the schools of thought concern this third usage of the terms. When we say that an action is *ḥusn* or good, we simply mean that it is praiseworthy in the sight of Allah and when we say that an action is *qubḥ* or ugly, we simply mean that the action is blameworthy. But how do we know the good from the bad? Does the intellect tell us what is good, or does the *sharīʿah* tell us? Historically there have been three competing views regarding this question: those of the *Ashʿarī*, *Māturīdī* and the *Muʿtazili* (Rationalist) schools of thought.

The Rationalists believed that actions themselves can have the attribute of good or evil. Further, they believed that this quality, once found within the action itself, can be known by the intellect. According to Taftāzānī, actions for the Rationalists were determined to be good or bad based on one of two things: either the essence or an attribute of the action. For example, the essence of lying is evil, whereas a lie that was told to bring two feuding parties together is deemed to be good due to the outcome produced by it.

Another important classification of actions, according to the

97 Maḥbūbī, *Tanqīḥ*, p. 325.

Rationalists, involves those actions known solely through the *sharīʿah*, like fasting on certain days of the year. The Rationalists' primary belief regarding good and evil is that it's the *ʿaql* that primarily determines this categorization of an action. Therefore, they felt that Allah had to order the rational good and prohibit the rational bad and went so far as to state that the intellect is the *ḥākim* that determines good and evil.

The Ashʿarī school of thought occupies the other end of the spectrum regarding *taḥsīn* (determining good) and *taqbīḥ* (determining bad). They held the position that *ḥusn* and *qubḥ* can only be known by the *sharīʿah*. The difference between them and the Rationalist school was that former felt that actions by themselves had no independent quality of good or bad. Good was only that which Allah ordained and commanded and bad was only that which Allah forbade. Secondly, they stated that if good actions were known solely by the intellect, a person should not be rewarded and praised for doing them. For them, the concept of reward and punishment was solely in relation to the divine command. Islam, Christianity, and Judaism all find their roots in the life and sacrifices of Ibrāhīm who is celebrated and praised by Allah in the Qur'ān, not because he was committed to performing actions that seemed to be rationally good, but because of his ability to ignore the apparent nature of an action, and realize that good and bad lie in the submission of one's intellect to Allah's command.

In his poetic and spiritual masterpiece *al-Mathnawī*, Jalāl al-Dīn al-Rūmī tells a story of a certain Sultan Maḥmūd, who one day decided to test the intelligence of his courtiers and ministers. Sultan Maḥmūd called together the officials of his government with the aim of testing their intelligence. He took out a pearl from his treasury and handed it to the Chief Minister and questioned him: "What is the value of this pearl? How much can it be sold for?" The Chief Minister replied, "Sir, this pearl is of great value. It is more valuable than two hundred donkeys laden with gold." The Sultan then ordered: "I command you to crush this pearl." The Chief Minister replied: "I will not destroy this valuable pearl. I have the welfare of your treasury at heart, and to crush this valuable gem would amount to disrespect on my part." The Sultan applauded him for his response and rewarded him with a royal robe of honor.

The Sultan then took the pearl from the Chief Minister and handed it to another of his court officials and asked him to determine what the value of the pearl was. He replied, "Sir, this precious pearl is more valuable than half of your kingdom. May God protect this pearl." The Sultan commanded him similarly to crush the pearl. He replied, "Sir, my hands cannot move to destroy this valuable pearl. To destroy this pearl would amount to enmity towards your treasury." The Sultan praised him profusely for his reply and rewarded him as well. In this manner, the Sultan called sixty-five officials from his government and each one of them followed the example set by the Chief Minister. The Sultan praised each one of them and rewarded them with a royal robe of honor.

After testing all the other officials, the Sultan now turned to a man named ʿIyād, handed him the pearl and said: "O ʿIyād, every one of my officials has seen this pearl. You also take a look at its radiant light and tell me, what is its value?" ʿIyād replied, "Sir, whatever value I am going to mention, this pearl will be worth much more than that." The Sultan ordered, "Quickly, crush this valuable gem into pieces." ʿIyād knew the Sultan's temperament and immediately realized that the Sultan was testing him. He broke the valuable pearl into pieces and did not pay any attention towards receiving any reward.

As soon as he broke the pearl into pieces, a great commotion ensued. The Chief Minister uttered, "By Allah! This man is a disbeliever, an ungrateful one, showing no regard for a valuable gem belonging to you, O Sultan!" ʿIyād replied, "Respected brothers! Which is more valuable, the command of the Sultan or this pearl? O people, in your sight the pearl is more valuable than the Sultan's command. I could not dismiss your command and, like a polytheist, turn towards the pearl. To remove my sight from the king and turn towards the pearl is equivalent to *shirk* in the love and obedience towards the king."

ʿIyād continued: "Respected sirs, is the command of the Sultan more valuable or the pearl? I shall not move my sight from the Sultan, and I will not turn my sight to the pearl like a polytheist. O you unworthy ones! The actual pearl was the Sultan's command! All of you broke the pearl of the Sultan's command." When ʿIyād explained this secret to the Ministers, they were humiliated and disgraced by his understanding.

Submission that involves ignoring the intellect when faced with revelation from Allah is what we would consider the true position of prophetic intelligence embodied by the Prophet Muḥammad ﷺ, thus earning him the title of "the most intelligent."

We are left with the last of the three competing schools of thought—the Māturīdī school. Like the Rationalists, the Māturīdī school felt that the good or bad nature of some actions could be known by looking at the essence of the action or an attribute of the action. They came to this view based on an objection of the Rationalists. They naturally objected to the idea that all good and evil was only known by the *sharīʿah* because this, according to them, led to circular reasoning. Their argument, as explained by Maḥbūbī, was that if the intellect could not know what was good and evil then "the necessity of believing in a prophet is dependent on the very message which a prophet himself brought."[98] Speaking the truth had to be known as good in and of itself in order for faith to be binding. Maḥbūbī explains that the Māturīdī response was to conclude that some actions are indeed recognized naturally by the intellect without depending on revelation; for example, the good nature of telling the truth and the evil nature of lying. Emphasis must be placed here that the Māturīdī position differs from that of the Rationalists in that the Rationalists believed that the *ʿaql* could determine the *ḥusn* and *qubḥ* of all actions whereas the Māturīdīs stated that this was only the case for some actions. A ninth-century work by Bābartī explains, in detail, the difference. He quotes directly from Ibn al-Qutlūbughā's commentary on *Masāyara*:

98 Maḥbūbī, *Tanqīḥ*, p. 328.

> The Māturīdī position is opposed to the Rationalist school in various ways. First, the Rationalists held that the ʿ*aql* could recognize good or bad in the action and reach the wisdom behind that nature independent of the *sharīʿah*. Whereas the Māturīdī position was that the ʿ*aql* could reach the good or bad nature of an action, but does not decide good or bad by itself at all, rather it must wait for the *sharīʿah* to decide. The ʿ*aql* was the decider for the Rationalist and a tool for explaining and discovering the wisdom for the Māturīdī.[99]

The second difference between the Māturīdī and Rationalist position, as explained by Ibn Qutlūbaghā is that,

> . . .the Māturīdīs did not reach the same necessary conclusion as the Rationalists regarding commanding the good being necessary for Allah and prohibiting evil being necessary upon Allah. According to the Ḥanafīyyah[100] the one mandating is solely Allah and the ʿ*aql* simply recognizes.[101]

The Māturīdī position that some actions are known as good, independent of revelation, seems to provide the balance needed for navigating this question, especially considering the long list of cognitive biases that have been discovered. The cognitive bias codex lists dozens of mistakes in judgment that the intellect routinely makes. While we have always been aware of the limitations of our cognitive faculties, we haven't had such extensive evidence for these limitations as we have today.

The struggle for Muslims of the postmodern era in many ways resembles the early debates over the authoritative nature of revelation when it seemingly clashed with the minds of their time. Today we struggle to convince ourselves of the high position of revelation when it clashes with the political pragmaticism of America and much

---

99 Bābartī, *Sharḥ Waṣiyyat al-Imām Abū Ḥanīfa*, p. 54.

100 The author is still speaking about the Māturidi when he uses the term *Hanafiyya* in this context. This is in reference to the great Imam Abū Hanifa.

101 Bābartī, *Sharḥ Waṣiyyat al-Imām Abū Ḥanīfa*, p. 54.

of the world. The political pragmatist argument pivots around one question, "Does it work?" They judge truth only based on the practical consequences of something. For them, truth is not an objective but rather a tool to solve a problem presented by life. Amongst educated Muslims, we are witnessing a rebirth of the Rationalists' understanding of the intellect, due to Scientism and modern philosophical and political thought. For the modern mind, when the intellect is in conflict with revelation the latter must be privatized and removed from the public discourse. The problem is that the desire of those who wished to free man from idiotic dogma and irrational social constructs blinded them from the shortsightedness and limited nature of the intellect.

Explaining why the Māturīdī position should be given preference over the Ashʿarī school, Ibn Qutlūbugha says,

> The difference between our position and the Ashʿarī position is that we say some actions are known to the *ʿaql* by Allah creating in it a knowledge. That knowledge can be by means of acquisition or inspired, even if the *sharīʿah* has not mentioned it. This is a necessary statement regarding those things which the *sharīʿah* depends on like the necessity of affirming the truthfulness of prophets and the evil nature of lying. This conclusion is necessary so that we don't succumb to the logical fallacy of circular reasoning.[102]

In verse 10 of Sūrah al-Mulk, the people destined for the Hellfire, regretfully say, "If only we had listened or understood, we would not be among the people of the blaze."[103] This verse answers an objection raised by the Ashʿarī school. One of the Ashʿarī arguments for good and evil being dependent on the *sharīʿah* was the verses of the Qur'ān stating that no nation would be punished before a messenger was sent to them. They stated that these verses clearly prove that the determining factor regarding praiseworthiness and blameworthiness was whether the messenger had communicated to a nation what was good and bad.

102 Bābartī, *Sharḥ Waṣiyyat al-Imām Abū Ḥanīfa*, p. 54.

103 Q 67:10.

However, this verse places responsibility for salvation on one of two things; "If only we used our *intellect* or *listened*," establishing that the intellect is responsible as well. Ibn al-Qayyim, in his encyclopedic work, *Miftāḥ*, describes those who have the strongest conviction as those who recognized, with their intellect, the goodness of the religion as a whole and the goodness found in each and every commandment of Allah. This too suggests that the *ʿaql* is not only responsible before Allah, but also that it is the greatest tool we have. In the words of Maḥbūbī, "according to us, Allah decides the good, and the *ʿaql* is the tool used to discover it. Allah creates a knowledge within the heart or *ʿaql* of a person after they attempt to use their *ʿaql correctly*."

MORAL BLINDNESS AND WEAKNESS

> And make mention of Our slaves Abraham, Isaac, and Jacob; men of power and insight.[104]

The first responsibility of the intellect is to know Allah and to see truth as truth and to see the falsehood as falsehood. Thereafter, the intellect must learn to "see" what is good for it and what is harmful for it. Throughout the Qur'ān, the theme of intellectual blindness is repeated often. In this section we will discuss at length the sight of the intellect from the perspectives of Ghazālī, Rāzi, and Muḥāsibī. Firstly, their understanding of the *ʿaql* provides us with an appreciation for the depth of early Islamic scholarship and secondly, a theoretical framework for understanding the role of the *ʿaql* in relation to revelation.

The first level of sight of the intellect is the basic knowledge of Allah's existence; in other words, to rationally deduce from creation that Allah is *wājib al-wujūd* or necessarily existent. Of course, this is an intrinsic aspect of moral intelligence because morality must be grounded in the heavens, just like our example of the inverted tower

104 Q 38:45.

of Babel. The next level of sight of the intellect is what we will coin "moral compass calibration." This is how we define what is correct and it is the first role of the ʿ*aql*. As we shall discuss in the coming chapters, moral intelligence consists of (a) the calibration of the moral compass; (b) establishment of moral commitment; (c) building moral sensitivity; (d) cultivating the grit for moral problem solving; and lastly (e) moral assertiveness. An inability in any of these capacities can be traced to a failure of the intellect to see correctly, or a weakness in the ʿ*aql* to determine a course of action. Knowledge of the truth and witnessing to the truth but failing to address life's problems by means of the truth, or unwillingness to assert one's moral subscriptions openly are also forms of weakness within the ʿ*aql*. In our construct of prophetic moral intelligence, the first aspect is calibration of the Moral Compass or establishment of the prophetic moral criterion. The second aspect of this moral intelligence is Moral Commitment. This capacity is behavioral and deficiencies in this area lead to mindless following of desires. The moral compass is knowledge-based, and ignoring it is caused by a sickness in the heart, which is the seat of the ʿ*aql*. Before we discuss the theme of blindness found in the Qur'ān in more detail, I would like to point out that, more often than not, a person may possess a working moral compass but it is simply not calibrated to revelation. This leads to incorrect judgments and leads a person astray unknowingly. This condition is discussed in the Qur'ān where Allah says, "Say: 'Shall we tell you whose works will bring the greatest loss?' Those whose efforts have been wasted in the life of the world while they thought they were doing good."[105]

A calibrated moral compass sees truth as truth and sees falsehood as falsehood. In contrast, the ʿ*aql* that is sick struggles to correctly identify or recognize right and wrong. Commenting on the ʿ*aql*'s inability to see accurately, Ibn al-Qayyim[106] draws a correlation between the tendency of a physical illness to alter perception and the perception of the heart:

105 Q 18:103–104

106 Ibn Qayyim al-Jawziyya, *Ighāthat al-Lahfān*, vol. 1, p. 21.

> Sometimes the sickness in the body removes one's perception completely, like blindness or paralysis, or one's perception is simply weakened, or it will completely mix things up like a person who tastes sweet things as bitter or vice versa.

A sick person may become nauseous when they smell fried food being prepared or, to use Ghazālī's example, to a sick person honey may taste bitter. We also see the same tendency regarding the body's perception of temperature during sickness. Ibn al-Qayyim explains that there is a symmetry between the health of the heart and the health of the body regarding perceiving things as they actually are. He explains that the very same condition (i.e., altered perception) can and does occur within the heart as well.

> His sickness (in the heart) is a type of imbalance, that throws off the intellect's ability to see truth and prevents one from intending to seek truth. Thus, the person no longer sees the truth as the truth, or he sees it other than what it is, or his ability to recognize it (truth) is weakened. So, he begins to hate the truth, which is actually beneficial, or love falsehood, which is harmful, very often both of these things happen at the same time.[107]

In Sūrah Taḥā, Allah provides a very powerful depiction of the Final Day and focuses on the theme of "blindness":

> But whosoever turns away from My remembrance, assuredly he will have a life of narrowness, and on the Resurrection Day We shall raise him up blind. He will say: "Why have You raised me up blind while I had sight [in my lifetime]?" He will say: "So [it must be] Our revelations came to you, but you disregarded them; so will you this day be disregarded."[108]

When these people question the reason their physical sight has been

---

107 Ibn Qayyim, al-Jawziyya, *Ighāthat al-Lahfān*, vol. 1, p. 15.

108 Q 20:124–126.

stripped away, they are told that the imposed blindness they are currently experiencing is a result of the voluntary choice they made to ignore the intellect's inclination to know Allah. Interestingly, another verse speaks about people in a similar situation on the day of judgment but suggests the exact opposite. While the aforementioned verse speaks of wicked people being blinded, this verse suggests that their sight will be made very sharp.

> And the Horn is blown. This is the threatened Day. Every soul will come, a driver with it and a witness. "You were heedless of this. Now We have removed your veil from you, so your sight this day is sharp."[109]

Why the apparent contradiction with the previous verse? It is commonly witnessed that when people lose one faculty, the brain often strengthens another to compensate for the loss. A person who becomes blind may begin to develop a sharp sense of touch or hearing. These two verses, when taken together, seem to highlight the dynamic connection between the physical sight and the sight of the *ʿaql*. We are told from the biography of the Prophet ﷺ that before revelation came to him and his spiritual sight was open to the ultimate extent he was "made to love solitude" and he would spend days on end alone inside a cave, away from the clamor of the city. Could it be that when we allow the physical means of learning (i.e., the eyes and ears) to be deprived of stimulation it results in the power of the heart strengthening? Or could it be that when the veils are lifted, the extreme intensity of light and information that floods into the heart causes the physical eye to feel blinded by the realities the heart is witnessing? This seems to be the opinion of Ghazālī. He explains, in his *Mishkāt al-Anwār,*[110] that just as sleep can allow one to see things which they can't in a wakeful state, "the senses [can] overpower the inner divine light." He explains that sleep, by its very nature, blocks the senses and as a result the inner

109 Q 50:20–22.

110 Ghazālī, *Miskhāt al-Anwār*, ʿĀlam al-Kutub, 1987.

divine light allows the heart to see that which it could not see while awake. More profound is the reality that the Prophet ﷺ was able to see with his heart while awake what others could only see while asleep. His inner eye was never blinded by the presence of the physical.

In order to gain a deeper understanding of the Qur'ānic themes of the removal of veils and sharp-sightedness (keen, acute vision) mentioned in the verses above, we must first take a closer look at the relationship between the intellect and physical sight. Perhaps one of the most profound explanations of this relationship can be found in Ghazālī's *Mishkāt al-Anwār*. Through his explanation of "the Light verse" we are provided a glimpse into the early understandings of the relationship between *ʿaql*, light, and sight. The depth of Ghazālī's understanding of the inner dimensions of being, along with his ability to explain the purpose, function, and relationships between the various God-given human faculties is simply profound.

OBSERVER VS. INSTRUMENT: THE CONNECTION BETWEEN EYESIGHT AND INSIGHT

In order to fulfill the responsibility of divine stewardship, human beings have been distinguished from the rest of Allah's creation with two types of sight which have often been metaphorically referred to as *nūr* (light). These two lights are the physical sight (*baṣar*) and insight (*baṣīrah*). Eyesight, explains Ghazālī has been metaphorically called light because it is dependent on an external source of light to perform its function. In the Qur'ān, we are reminded of this weakness and perpetual dependency on external light to navigate the world around us, lest we take our sight for granted. Allah asks mankind,

> Say: "Have you thought, if Allah made night everlasting for you till the Day of Arising; what god besides Allah will bring you light? Will you not then hear?" Say: "Have you thought, if Allah made day everlasting for you till the Day of Arising; what god besides

> Allah will bring you night wherein you rest? Will you not see?" Of His mercy has He appointed for you night and day, that you may rest therein, that you may seek of His favors, and that you may be thankful.[111]

Ghazālī explains that, in reality, it is the *baṣīrah* of the *ʿaql* that is far more deserving of the metaphoric title of light than physical sight. While the eye is dependent on light to see things, the *ʿaql* is uniquely able to both illuminate and perceive. It is the role of the intellect to make the unknown known, to make that which was hidden from us visible. The eye doesn't make things visible; it can only see what has already been made visible by light. The *ʿaql* can actually make things known that were, prior to rational thought and deduction, unknown. It illuminates the unknown. As I read this point of Ghazālī, I could not help but remember the cartoons we used to watch as children. When a character had an idea, a lightbulb would illuminate above their head.

Explaining the details of light, Ghazālī continues,

> In relation to sight, things will fall into one of three categories: that which is dark and hence impossible to see; those things that are visible but do not illuminate other things like distant stars and burning embers; and lastly, those things that are not only visible but also illuminate other things as well, like the sun, a lamp, or the moon.[112]

One's ultimate goal and highest achievement is not to become like stars to be gazed upon, but rather to become a lamp or even the sun whose light gives benefit to people and animals. From his analysis we understand that the *ʿaql* is more deserving of the noble title of *nūr* because it falls into the third category of things that illuminate other things like the sun, the moon, or a lamp. Before we move on to discuss how physical sight and intellectual conception relate to one another, I feel we should look a bit closer at this statement.

111 Q 28:71–73.

112 Ghazālī, *Miskhāt al-Anwār*, p. 120.

Ghazālī provides us with multiple ways that *baṣīrah* is different than *baṣar.* The first, and perhaps most profound, difference between the *baṣar* and the *baṣīrah* is that the physical eye, unlike the intellect, cannot perceive itself. Rather, it is not aware of its own ability to see. He says, "The eye cannot perceive itself while the *ʿaql* can perceive itself and perceive other things as well."[113] He further explains, "It can not only perceive itself, but it is aware of its knowledge of itself and its knowledge of its knowledge *ad infinitum*. This is not the case with the physical eye."

As we mentioned before, this is the primary way in which humans have been divinely preferred over animals. In other words, it is consciousness that has placed mankind in the position of the most distinguished of creation. Human metacognition is what allows us to be witnesses of Allah's creation and why testifying to the Oneness of Allah is the ultimate purpose of our creation. I am not suggesting here that other creatures don't witness the Singularity and Divinity of Allah. We are told throughout the Qur'ān that all of creation praises and glorifies Allah. But what we aren't told is whether or not the rest of creation can understand their ability to perceive. Can they conceptualize their conceptualization? Let's suppose that you are standing before a beautiful mountain range, looking at the splendid colors and the texture of the land. You take out your binoculars to take a closer look. Are the binoculars that you are looking through aware of what they are looking at? Can they marvel at its beauty? Can they deduce the existence of a Creator? Of course they cannot. They are a tool whose purpose is to magnify distant objects. The eyes also see the mountain range but they, like the binoculars, are simply the means. The *ʿaql* is the only faculty created by Allah that can see and value what it sees. It is not the only thing that can *become* a witness to the greatness of Allah's creation but rather the only thing that can *bear* witness. The Prophet ﷺ once said to his Companions, "You are God's witnesses

113 Ghazālī, *Miskhāt al-Anwār*, p. 121.

on earth." The greatest level of existence is not only to bear witness, but to live in a state of perpetual awareness of witnessing. The *ʿaql* is uniquely distinguished because it alone functions as both a tool of observation and a witness.

Ibn Sīnā takes this point to a deeper level. He explains that "Each faculty, which perceives through an instrument, does not perceive itself, nor its instrument, nor its act of perception." Like Ghazālī, Ibn Sīnā is saying that the eye cannot see itself, nor can it conceptualize sight. Only the *ʿaql* has this capacity. It is a tool that, when trained or divinely blessed, has the ability to step outside of itself and perceive itself and its act of seeing, just as a person who lights a candle in a dark room immediately gains knowledge of the room and anything in it. They also, and perhaps more importantly, become aware of themselves. Our capacity to observe ourselves within the cosmos is what gives us the ability to fulfill the divine role of stewardship or *khilāfa*.

The second difference between the *baṣar* and the *baṣīrah*, according to Ghazālī, is that, "The eye cannot see that which is far away or that which is extremely close, while the *ʿaql* is not affected by distance; the far and near are equally visible and can be conceived. It can ascend to the highest parts of the universe and to the depths of the earth."

The third difference is that the *baṣar* cannot see beyond a partition, while the *ʿaql* can go beyond a partition and conceptualize[114] the throne of Allah, the *kursī*, and beyond the seven heavens.

The fourth difference between *baṣar* and *baṣīrah*, according to Ghazālī, is that "the eye can only see the outward aspect of things. The physical eye cannot perceive the inner aspect of things, while the *ʿaql* can dive into the depths of things beyond the external to its secrets and reach the inner reality of those things. It can understand cause and effect and it can understand the intent of existence. It can

114 Of course, the conceptualization of these things is mere intellectual comprehension. These things are in the realm of the unseen; they are "behind the Partition." While the eye is completely ignorant of that which is beyond the partition, the *ʿaql*, after receiving information regarding what is beyond the partition, can possess knowledge of it.

deduce what a thing is made of, how a thing was made, and why a thing was made." Here, Ghazālī highlights the inherently superficial and shallow nature of physical sight. The person who begins to look at the creation through the *ʿaql* begins to appreciate inner beauty and perfection in contrast to external beauty and perfection. When we look holistically at the Prophet's teachings, we see that he was constantly encouraging humanity to close the *baṣar* and look through the *baṣīrah.* While humanity currently finds itself in the selfie age, predominantly preoccupied with the external form, the Prophet's teachings reminds us that the focal point of Divine concern is inner form and the soundness of one's heart. In one narration, the Prophet ﷺ said, "Indeed Allah does not look at your physical form and your wealth but rather he looks at your heart and your actions."[115] This narration reminds mankind what really matters. As a noun, the word "matter" is defined as a physical substance in general, *as distinct from mind and spirit* (i.e., matter is visible to the eye.) In the verbal form, matter is defined "to be of importance; have significance." The collective Islamic ethos emphasizes that what matters is actually what is within the human (i.e., the mind and the spirit.) Perhaps it is language that is shaping our worldview since the prophetic teachings tell us that matter is not what ultimately matters. We find in a tradition that the Prophet Muḥammad ﷺ taught his followers to recite a specific supplication upon seeing one's reflection in a mirror: "O Allah, just as you have beautified my external form, please beautify my internal form!" Perhaps Allah's insistence on covering our physical forms is in truth a means for humanity to open its spiritual eye, whilst the modern obsession with revealing the body is simply an attempt to divert our attention from our unattractive, inner realities.

The fifth difference, according to Ghazālī, is that the physical eye can only perceive a small portion of the creation since it cannot perceive the objects of the mind and misses many of the sensually

115 Muslim, *Ṣaḥīḥ Muslim*, vol. 4, p. 1986.

perceived things. It also is blind to the inner qualities of the self, such as happiness, pain, worry, grief, joy, desire, and knowledge. "Its scope is extremely narrow because it cannot go beyond color and form,"[116] explains Ghazālī. While performing his sacred pilgrimage, Malcolm X wrote back to his brethren in America explaining that he felt like Islam could solve the race problem in America. The more we look at people through our eyes and not our hearts, the more susceptible we are to shallow superficial judgments. Conversely, if we work to open and expand the perception of the heart, we will begin to perceive the deeper realities of those around us. This fifth point also highlights a central theme of this book, namely, that it is the *ʿaql* that perceives and understands emotion.

Lastly, Ghazālī points out that the physical sight makes many mistakes regarding the physical nature of the things it sees. For example, an airplane flying forty thousand feet above looks small, but we know it is much larger than it appears. Ghazālī claims, "The types of errors made by the eyes are many yet the *ʿaql* is free from those errors."[117] But what about the mistakes the intellect makes? What about the misjudgments made by people every day? Ghazālī ends this section by presenting the hypothetical questions I have just mentioned and explains that proper usage of the *ʿaql* is free of mistakes and incorrect judgments. He says that all the mistakes of the intellect have been explained and clarified in his two books, *Miʿyār al-ʿilm* and *Miḥakk al-Naẓar*, both of which are books on logic. According to Ghazālī, it is inconceivable for the intellect to fall into error when it is freed from false and baseless thoughts. Just as a person trained in grammar is expected not to fall into grammatical error, the one trained in logic is expected not to fall victim to fallacious arguments or thinking. If the grammarian happens to make a mistake, it is quite simple for someone to point it out and thereby rectify it. When the intellect is trained, it will perceive things

116 Ghazālī, *Miskhāt al-Anwār*, p. 123.

117 Ghazālī, *Miskhāt al-Anwār*, p. 127.

exactly as they are. Likewise, its vision will become even sharper at the time of death when the veils are completely lifted.

LIGHT UPON LIGHT

> Allah is the Light of the heavens and earth. The likeness of His Light is that of a niche in which is a Lamp. The Lamp is in a glass, the glass, is as it were a glittering star, lit from a blessed tree, an olive, neither of the east, nor of the west, whose oil would almost glow forth, even if no fire touched it, light upon light. Allah guides whom He wills to His light and gives examples to the people; and Allah knows everything.[118]

At this point I would like to revisit Ghazālī's discussion regarding the eyes' dependence upon external light. It offers profound insight into the nature of our relationship with revelation. He explains that, just as the eye is dependent upon external light to see, the *ʿaql* is dependent on an external light source. This means that, while the *ʿaql* is a light in and of itself, capable of illuminating other things for its possessor, it is not the source of the light itself. This is similar to the light of the moon which reflects the light of the sun brilliantly, guiding those who wish to benefit from it. What then is the external light that the intellect depends on? Before we answer that question, it seems appropriate to highlight one implication of the reality of the intellect's light. Just as the physical inability to see could be due to an absence of external light or due to one simply closing their eyes, the inability of the *ʿaql* to see can be the natural consequence of something blocking its external source of light or simply because a person has failed to open the eye of the intellect and use this amazing faculty.[119] And just as the sharpness and accuracy of physical sight increases when sunlight is

118 Q 24:35.

119 Also, see section on Logic.

present, so too does the *ʿaql*'s acumen and sharpness amplify when its light source is amplified.

The logical conclusion of all types of dependency for the atheist is infinite regress. Each domino in an endless row of falling dominoes earns its turn to fall due to the one that preceded it. This, of course, will continue forever unless there is some force, other than the dominoes that exist out of the chain, to end the process. In the case of the eye, traditionally its dependency on light ultimately goes back to one source, the sun. It is a source that does not need to gain its light from somewhere else. The chain of physical light stops there. But what about the light of the *ʿaql*? What is the ultimate source of its illuminating capacity? It must be a source that is outside of the chain and it must be ultimate. Allah tells us beautifully that He is the ultimate source of the light of the heavens and the earth, and that revelation is the light which allows the *ʿaql* to see correctly. The "light upon light" referenced in this verse is the light of revelation guiding the light of the intellect.

FRAMEWORK FOR MORAL INTELLIGENCE

When describing the role of the intellect, Ghazālī uses the example of a rider on horseback. He says that the rider represents the intellect and the horse represents a person's body and their desires. Ideally, the rider should know where they want to go; they should have a goal or destination in mind. Beyond having a goal or destination, the rider should also know how to get to that place or have a map to guide them. The complete moral intelligence that was inspired into the heart and intellect of the Prophet ﷺ provides humanity with the knowledge of where they should be trying to go, how they should get there, how to stay on the path and how to solve the problems they will face while attempting to reach that destination. We have broken down moral intelligence into five distinct capacities. A complete moral education serves to develop each of these five areas.

Our proposed framework for the moral intelligence of the Prophet

ﷺ serves as a model and guide for parents and educators who find it difficult to figure out why their children aren't making correct moral judgments. We often don't know where to begin when we speak about moral and spiritual development. This framework for moral intelligence provides parents and educators with a fundamental understanding of the most essential aspect of the Prophet's intelligence—the moral aspect. This is what I believe will develop your children's moral identity and define who they are. In the Qur'ān Allah says, "Who is better in speech than the one who calls others to Allah while they themselves do righteous actions and say, 'I am a Muslim?'"[120] This verse offers us a deeper appreciation for the primacy of establishing a moral identity that is aligned with the prophetic moral standard. The verse begins by pointing out important aspects of being a Muslim: first, calling others to Allah; second, performing righteous deeds yourself; and third, establishing an understanding of who you are. What I find unique about this verse is the order in which these things are mentioned. My personal reflection on this verse is that the last thing mentioned (i.e., Muslim identity) is what is shaped first. Then, after developing that identity, a person attempts to act in ways that are consistent with who they are. Lastly, they then develop an empathic desire for others to know Allah and live by this way as well. Developing our children's moral identity is achieved first by understanding the framework of moral intelligence and thereafter working to developing each of its five capacities.

Prophetic moral intelligence involves the holistic knowledge, control, and courage necessary for fulfilling the role of divine stewardship or *Khilāfah.* The pedagogical aids needed to pass this intelligence to others will be discussed in the sections covering emotional intelligence and change. This section will present and describe the framework of moral intelligence. When we discuss the intelligence of the Prophet ﷺ, we are looking at the knowledge of *what* he was given by Allah and

120 Q 41:33.

the knowledge of *how* to pass that to others. Together, they are the most essential aspects of divine stewardship.

FIVE ASPECTS OF MORAL INTELLIGENCE

Our theory regarding moral education focuses on five key aspects of moral intelligence. Our understanding is that the further away one gets from the Prophet's era, the more each of these areas has been attacked and undermined. To protect one's intelligence, one must recognize that prioritizing these aspects is vital to one's spiritual life and well-being. We have listed the five capacities in their hierarchical order.

1. A Moral Compass that is calibrated to the prophetic ideals;
2. Conviction and commitment to following those ideals;
3. Moral Sensitivity or the ability to recognize right from wrong;
4. Moral Problem solving or the ability to apply moral reasoning to problems that arise in life; and
5. Moral Assertiveness or the courage to promote and defend that which is right.

Accurate moral compass calibration is the foundation of the model of prophetic intelligence and thus the most important to learn and protect. The other four capacities are used to support and confirm the direction and guidance provided by the moral compass. According to our model, moral assertiveness and moral commitment are only praiseworthy when they are connected to a prophetically calibrated moral compass. These five aspects only begin to outline the divinely inspired and complex moral intelligence bestowed upon the Prophet ﷺ and passed on to his followers. It is hoped that more thorough investigation into the moral intelligence of the Prophet ﷺ will inspire a massive shift in the culturally dominant understanding of Moral Education.

Allah sent his prophets and messengers with the objective of eradicating the darkness of moral ignorance from the individual human intellect and the collective society. The time before, or between, the advent of a prophet or messenger is appropriately called the "days of ignorance" since the moral compass of humanity, in the absence of divine revelation, cannot provide sufficient guidance. As we mentioned before, the *ʿaql* can only see correctly when it has the proper external light. That external light is the revelation of Allah. Those who come to, or back to, Islam often refer to the time before they were guided as the "days of ignorance" as well because of the absence of divine guidance. A proper moral education provides believers with the foundation and confidence needed to remain steadfast and committed. It teaches the believer how to live by those ideals and how to solve life's complex problems, be they individual or collective, without sacrificing the moral standard of Allah. A moral education also provides the believer with clear proofs regarding the fallacy of disbelief so that Muslims can regain their place as the rightful flag bearers of intelligence and rationality.

MORAL COMPASS

The vanguard of moral intelligence is having a moral compass that is calibrated to prophetic ideals. Its calibration is the first goal of a moral education because in order for behavioral changes to be authentic they must be preceded by cognitive changes. Thereafter, a person is able to regulate and evaluate their own actions and the actions of others. The first goal of a moral education can be found within an exchange that took place between the Prophet ﷺ and a Companion by the name of Wābiṣah.

> Wābiṣah the son of Maʿbad narrated that the Prophet once said to him. "You have come to ask about morality and immorality?" "Yes, I have." The Prophet clenched his fist and hit me on my chest above my heart and said, "Ask yourself! Ask your heart, Wābiṣah! Ask yourself! Ask your heart, Wābiṣah! Ask yourself! Ask your heart,

> Wābiṣah!" repeating it three times for emphasis. "Piety consists of those actions that put your soul in a tranquil state and do the same to your heart, while immoral actions are those things that scratch at your heart and prevent it from being in a state of rest and peace even if the jurists inform you that such and such action is permitted."[121]

When a person has developed a strong moral compass, the letter of the law does little to provide them with inner peace. In this exchange, we find the Prophet ﷺ, who has knowledge of all that is good and bad, telling Wābiṣah to ask his own heart. It is important to remember that, from the Qur'ānic perspective the *ʿaql* is found within the heart. By shifting the burden of responsibility back upon the heart of Wābiṣah, the Prophet ﷺ is informing all of the Muslims that it is their responsibility to calibrate their heart's moral compass. At the end of this narration, the Prophet ﷺ tells Wābiṣah to follow his heart's inclination regardless of what *fatwa* or legal verdict he is given. This, in my estimation, is a clear indication that a person's ultimate goal should not only be to learn and know the law, but to live by its spirit. This, then, will be your guide. It is essential that we understand that he said this to a Companion whose moral compass he knew was calibrated. For others whose hearts were not yet calibrated, he did not tell them to follow their heart because in that case they would be misguided. For those individuals, he worked on calibrating them.

The practical steps for calibrating the moral compass are:

1. Keeping the company of the righteous;
2. Recitation of the Qur'ān with understanding and contemplation;
3. Studying the life of the Prophet ﷺ;
4. Making humble supplications before Allah;
5. Learning the law and forcing oneself to live by it; and
6. Repenting to Allah and avoiding sin.

---

121 Mundhirī, *al-Targhīb wa al-Tarhīb*, vol. 2, p. 351.

Remember that, although sins are lapses in the moral commitment of the heart, they have a direct effect on the cognitive insights of the *ʿaql*. Living according to the commands of Allah, to the best of one's ability, causes an increase in and sharpening of the *ʿaql's* cognitive ability. Regarding this Allah says, "O you who believe! If you fear Allah, He will give you discrimination [between right and wrong] and will remit from you your sins and forgive you. Allah's grace is tremendous."[122]

This *furqān,* or criterion, is one's moral compass. It is the means by which the good and bad are recognized. ʿUmar ibn al-Khaṭṭāb was known as al-Fārūq, or the distinguisher between truth and false, because his moral compass was permanently set to the most upright prophetic ideal.

Just as a navigational compass is affected by a strong enough presence, a person's moral compass can also be negatively influenced. A compass uses the magnetic field of the earth to inform which direction is north. However, if a smaller magnet is brought in close proximity of a compass, this tiny magnet will throw off the compass despite the overwhelmingly massive magnetic field of the earth. A person's moral compass is affected by negative company in the same way. When one keeps the company of people whose hearts are calibrated to things other than the prophetic ideal, they will notice their compass begins to misguide them. For this reason the Prophet ﷺ said, "A man is on the religion of his closest companions. So be wary of the company you keep."[123]

MORAL COMMITMENT

One's Moral commitment refers to their ability to live by the moral ideals they subscribe to. Within the framework of moral intelligence, we are placing it second only to calibrating the moral compass.

While our moral compass does have the function of telling us which

122 Q 8:29.

123 Abū Dawūd, *Sunan Abī Dawūd*, vol. 4, p. 259.

direction is correct, it has nothing to do with the actions we choose. Moral commitment, on the other hand, is a behavioral capacity focused on producing within believers the will-power to live according to those ideals. A rational, moral subscription to a set of ideals, though absolutely necessary for calibrating our moral compass, is not sufficient to effect moral commitment. The actions we choose to engage in are the result of many factors. For example, more often than not, habit and emotion play a much larger role than our moral subscriptions, even if those moral subscriptions are rational and authentic. For this reason, moral commitment is arguably one of the most cited themes in the Qur'ān and literature on Islamic ethics. Moral commitment takes strength of the heart, not knowledge. In the Qur'ān, we find Allah repeatedly reminding the Prophet Muḥammad ﷺ about the level of commitment displayed by other prophets in the face of opposition. Hence, we are told that the reason these stories were mentioned so frequently to the Prophet ﷺ was so, in the words of Allah, "that we could strengthen your heart."[124] In this chapter we discuss how to strengthen the heart and the *ʿaql* enough to follow what it knows to be correct. Moral commitment is difficult, and this is undoubtedly an understatement.

Ibn Abbās[125] tells us that the heaviest verse revealed upon the Prophet ﷺ was, "Stay committed as you have been ordered."[126] Imam al-Qurṭubī narrates that the companion Abū ʿAli al-Sirrī saw the Prophet ﷺ in a dream and asked him, "O Prophet of Allah, it is reported that you said, 'Sūrat al-Hūd has given me grey hair.' What in that Sūrah is it that gave you grey hair? Is it the stories of the prophets? Is it the destruction of the previous nations?" The Prophet of Allah ﷺ replied, "No, it is the verse of Allah, 'Stay committed as you have been ordered.'" The Prophet ﷺ understood the gravity of the command for consistent commitment to the message. In another narration, the

124 Q 25: 32.

125 Qurṭubī, *Tafsīr Qurṭubī*, vol. 9, p. 107.

126 Q 11: 112.

Prophet ﷺ was asked by a Companion for comprehensive advice to which he replied, "Say, 'I believe in Allah' and then stay committed to that." Here, again, we see the cognitive element of the *ʿaql* followed by the behavioral element, in this case moral commitment, combining the sight and ability of the *ʿaql*.

On one occasion, the Prophet Muḥammad ﷺ delivered a powerful sermon, the eloquence of which moved the attendees to tears. One of the companions of the Prophet ﷺ said, "It is as if this is a farewell speech. Please give us some parting advice." The Prophet ﷺ replied, "Hold on to my way and the way of my pious successors. Hold on to this way with your molar teeth."[127] In the early years of Prophethood when the Prophet Muḥammad ﷺ was asked by his beloved uncle to stop spreading his message, he replied with tears in his eyes, "I cannot." So how did the Prophet ﷺ inculcate this aspect of the prophetic intellect in his successors?

DEVELOPING MORAL COMMITMENT

There are countless narrations that address the virtue of moral commitment. What we intend to do is point out three elements found in a morally committed person. By identifying these elements, we hope to be able to create educational programs that work to develop each of these areas individually. Once these areas are developed, it is hoped that, with the help of Allah, the person will be morally committed. The three components needed for strong moral commitment are:

1. Certainty
2. Optimism
3. Unity

127 Tirmidhī, *Sunan al-Tirmidhī*, vol. 4, p. 341.

Certainty

The first element needed for strong moral commitment is certainty regarding one's moral subscriptions. This means that the person must have conviction that the things they are morally subscribed to are, in fact, the truth. Certainty, of course, is not a behavioral capacity of the *ʿaql* but rather a cognitive one directly relating back to the *baṣirah* of the intellect and calibration of the moral compass. As a person works to strengthen their certainty in the message and the guidance given to the Prophet ﷺ, they will necessarily find it much easier for them to stay committed to the prophetic moral standard.

Optimism

After a person has been convinced about the truth of their moral subscriptions, they should work to remove all negative emotions surrounding their ability to live by those ideals. A person must be encouraged to remain positive and optimistic about their own strength and the help of Allah. The first way that I suggest we build optimism is through beneficial company and a focused education on *rajā'* (hope) in Allah. Also, being in the presence of people who have successfully achieved a sought-after goal inspires us to feel that we too can reach that goal. The psychological effect of company works with all goals and objectives, be they academic, physical, or spiritual. The problem is that many of us don't have those types of examples around us to observe directly. For those of us who do not have righteous models around us to learn from, we should read about the lives of the righteous people of the past. One of the wisdoms behind the stories of the prophets being told so often to the Prophet Muḥammad ﷺ was that they gave him relatable examples of others who went through the same difficulties as he did and persevered. Sufyān ibn ʿUyanna used to say, "When the righteous people's names are mentioned, a special mercy of Allah descends."[128] The effect of that mercy is that the

128 Muḥāsibī, *Risālat al-Mustarshidīn*, p. 13.

ʿaql is strengthened. Normally a person will lose hope for one of two reasons: either they see themselves as too low and unworthy of what they are striving for or they see the objective as beyond their reach. Both of these are considered tricks of Shayṭān and need to be actively counteracted. By studying the concept of hope in books of Islamic spirituality, one develops a strong sense of why hope and optimism are natural, necessary elements of faith.

Unity

The last component involves identifying oneself with one's moral ideals, meaning that one sees their moral subscription as an intrinsic part of who they are. Moral subscription refers to a person believing a particular moral code to be correct and living by it. There are many reasons a person may subscribe to a moral code, such as societal or familial pressure or conformity with cultural norms. Ideally, the basis for moral subscription should be rational. This does not mean that a person must understand all of the reasoning behind all aspects of that moral code but that one has arrived at the decision to adopt that moral code rationally. When a person is "unified" with their moral code they do not see moral choices as exercises in sacrifice but rather they see their moral goals as part of who they are. There is absolute unity between them and their moral standards. When a person becomes unified with their moral judgments, a strong moral identity is formed, and these individuals are often the most inspiring people. Without unity, a person's moral judgments are always compromised on some level because they aren't completely attached to the person's identity.

MORAL SENSITIVITY, MORAL PROBLEM SOLVING AND MORAL COURAGE

Moral education primarily revolves around teaching someone how to apply moral idioms to actions and behaviors correctly. Moral idioms are those words we use to make value judgments every day of our lives. When we see someone standing out of respect for an elderly person, we connect a particular positive idiom to that action, perhaps "kind," "nice," or "thoughtful." Prior to moral education, children don't know how to label the feelings of jealousy or anger. They don't know how to categorize something as bad even though they can identify that something is not as it should be. Islamically speaking, it is the duty of the parent to teach their child how to appropriately label the moral quality of an action. If they fail to do so, popular culture will teach children how to see the world.

At an elementary level, a person should learn how to independently apply the correct idiom to the outer form of their own actions and behaviors as well as the actions and behaviors of others. A child should be able to distinguish between good and bad behavior. This level of education prepares them to move forward toward fulfilling the role of *khalīfah*. After all, that is the ultimate goal of prophetic teaching: to bring humanity to the level of divine stewardship. This educational process has no endpoint. Rather it simply becomes more and more critical of the inner forms of the actions and behaviors that take place. At this level, a person develops the ability to even distinguish between good actions. They can assess the inner objective and intention behind the action and truly judge the moral nature of the action. As we move further away from the prophetic era and closer to the end-times, we have been informed that people will not simply lose the ability to morally judge, but rather, they replace the divine standard of judgment with a satanic one. The words "good" and "bad" will not be lifted from the dictionaries of the world, but rather, the objects to which they should be connected to will be reversed. Moral relativism will usher in this satanic reversal because the word *good* must be separated from that which is good before it can be assigned to evil. The word *good* must lose meaning before a new meaning is given to it. This process is called *Moral Ambivalence,* we will discuss in the coming sections.

Moral sensitivity can, however, be developed with both breadth and depth. The breadth of moral sensitivity involves realizing that a moral idiom, such as courage, may have countless forms across many different cultures. This breadth of moral understanding without depth can lead to a form of relativism which completely strips moral idioms of any meaning. Depth in moral understanding gives a person the ability to see the common ground across cultures. Depth is also the inward-directed understanding of the moral idioms in a search for their deeper meaning. According to John Kekes, depth is not taught, but rather involves an individual's effort to see moral situations as others would see them.[129] Moral sensitivity is a crucial ability to accurately perceive the moral dimensions of the situation they are in. This perception is built and developed by learning moral idioms and developing breadth and depth in one's understanding of them. Moral idioms are, by nature, evaluative. The person using them must pass judgment on the situations in which they are employed. Moral idioms are also action-guiding because they tell us how we ought to act in a given situation.

In France, just days before I penned this chapter, an Algerian woman was denied French citizenship because she refused to shake hands with an unrelated man because of her moral identity. For this she was denied the "privilege" of a French citizenship. Why is it that a country that bears the flag of liberal values and enlightenment feels the need to regulate moral judgments and values? Without the shadow of a doubt, increasingly "progressive" societal trends have thrown a deadly left hook at the prophetic ideal of moral intelligence, causing our religious identity and our knees to buckle. But we need not lean against the ropes.

Over the last few years, I have become increasingly interested in studying the major societal trends in thought regarding ethics and morality over the last two centuries. My intention is perhaps best

129 Kekes, *The Morality of Pluralism.*

articulated by an Arab poet who said, "I study evil not for evil itself but rather to protect myself from it."

It is with the intent to protect myself and others from the intellectual and cultural trends within our society that seek to uproot the foundations of faith that I present the following discussion on a very fundamental aspect of our religious and moral identity and the threats posed against it. We mustn't throw in the towel, so to speak, due to the aggressive nature of these attacks, but rather we should put up our guard, study the strengths and weaknesses of our opponents closely and, with precision, strike accordingly. As inheritors and representatives of the Prophet ﷺ, it is our duty to continue the prophetic mission of building both individual and collective moral intelligence within our communities.

MORAL SENSITIVITY

Moral sensitivity is the *ʿaql*'s version of a lane departure warning. I recently rented a Toyota Camry and was completely caught off guard as the car automatically realigned my steering wheel when I began to drift outside of my lane. I remember when this feature first began to appear in cars, the car would simply notify the driver that they were moving out of their lane. Now we have reached the point where not only will basic sedans automatically adjust your steering wheel, but some cars can drive you all the way to work or school without you having to do anything at all. Moral sensitivity is that annoying beeping sound informing you that you are doing something wrong. We should also understand that these warning notifications and steering wheel correction systems can only work if the computer assumes that driving within one lane is the ideal and drifting from lane to lane is wrong and potentially harmful. Even our ability to drive ourselves to and from places is based on a collective agreement with, and a commitment to, a set of shared principles, like stopping at red lights and other commonly understood laws of the road. When a person switches lane without using their signal, we become upset because they have breached the shared principles; thus, we honk our horn. I think we can all agree that shared systems function smoothly due to each member of the system sharing the same rules.

Moral sensitivity is directly related to the moral idioms available to a person. The list of terms associated with moral approval includes: forthright, unassuming, generous, faithful, honorable, considerate, trustworthy, modest, courageous, honest, pure, and conscientious. The list of terms connoting moral condemnation includes: corrupt, cruel, treacherous, envious, petty, hypocritical, selfish, greedy, cowardly, obsequious. These are provided by language, tradition, and culture. A sound moral education involves teaching people which moral idiom to apply to which situation. When a person can apply these idioms to the situations they encounter, and even to themselves, their moral education is complete. When a person learns the meanings of these words (i.e., the moral idioms) and then learns the actions to which they are attributed, they develop a moral identity, or in other words a moral ideal, which they themselves may or may not reach but nonetheless remains the ideal.

AMBIVALENCE AND MORAL IDENTITY

Zygmunt Bauman, in *Modernity and Ambivalence,* explains the crux of moral ignorance: a state of cultural ambivalence. Simply put, he explains that ambivalence is a language disorder in which we fail to name things. It is "the possibility of assigning an object or an event to more than one category."[130] Think of a small child to whom you are teaching basic words. "This is big" or "This is small" teaches the child a word that can be used in the future to classify, segregate or differentiate between various things. Likewise, the statement, "This is an animal" provides the mind of the child with a mental box within which

130 Bauman, *Modernity and Ambivalence*, p. 2.

other animals can be placed. Bauman explains that we naturally and rightfully feel a sense of anxiety when confronted by ambivalence. In my estimation, this is because people like for things to fit neatly into categories and they are troubled by things that fall into the *grey areas*.

In the beginning of the Qur'ān, we are told about the creation of Adam and the initial education he received. The Qur'ān recounts that Adam was taught the "names of everything."[131] This hints at a human ability to categorize the world and subsequently learn from that world. When children are very young the most common question is, "What is that?" Only after building a basic vocabulary can children then ask the question, "Why?" This verse indicates that mankind has the ability to know things, name them, and thereby classify them and this constitutes the hallmark of human intellectual ability and the role of the *ʿaql*. The problem with modernity, as explained by Bauman, is that we have shifted into a state of collective ambivalence. Words like *generous, faithful, honorable, considerate, trustworthy, modest, courageous, honest,* and *pure* fail to classify actions, and therefore chaos, or as he puts it, "the other of order," ensues. Bauman's views seem to echo the sentiments of C.S. Lewis who said that moral relativism "will certainly end our species and damn our souls." The rational human mind inclines toward order and abhors chaos. When our language loses meaning and enters a chaotic state, when we are all speaking the same words but saying drastically different things, when we allow language, the very thing that distinguishes us from the beast, to be subjective, we have surely approached the fall of man. To a child, words have meaning, but for the "enlightened" postmodern mind, words mean nothing, or anything, or everything.

131 Q 2:31.

MORAL IDENTITY AND SHAME: TWO SIDES OF THE SAME COIN

Once a moral ideal has been formed within the *ʿaql* of a person, any subsequent failure to meet that ideal should naturally produce a sense of shame or *ḥayāʾ* within them. A mature and justified shame plays an important positive role for the person who experiences it and holds a central position in the moral sphere of the individual and the broader society. In one narration, the Prophet ﷺ defined shame as the single most identifying characteristic of Islam. "Every religion has a distinguishing characteristic and for Islam, that characteristic is a sense of shame."

Another narration attributed to the Prophet Sulaymān (peace and blessings be upon him) defines shame as "the string of the necklace of faith," suggesting that an individual's loss of shame destroys his or her religious identity.

Shame's central role in the moral intelligence sphere is directly connected to identity. The feeling of shame begins when one believes that they have failed to meet their own ideal. It forces a person to reexamine their moral identity and reconsider their closeness to that moral ideal, and it informs them about the weaknesses in their moral character. The powerful corrective effect of shame on behavior has even led some academics to suggest that the American justice system should employ shame instead of imprisonment. Islam, being a religion that is concerned with creating a culture of God-consciousness, takes shame as its defining characteristic. As the Prophet ﷺ informed us, "If you have no shame, you will do whatever you like." The problem with shame, according to Bernard Williams in *Shame and Necessity*, is that it is a very social emotion and thereby far too dependent on one's environment. Shame, by definition, can make a person a victim of the norms of the environment they live in. Doesn't this negate the potential benefit of shame? Shame's dependence on the communal gaze has led many people to feel that it is too dependent on society to be given primacy in an individual's moral sphere. People often feel ashamed for things they should not feel ashamed about because of the moral standards of the society they live in.

Minorities, women, the disabled, and menial and low-wage workers may feel an unwarranted sense of shame which is clearly the result of the ethos of the culture they live in. In other words, shame is far too heteronomous to be a good indicator of one's moral character. The proponents of this argument hold that true morality must be more autonomous, coming from within a person. Before I deconstruct this view, it should be noted that the Islamic definition of shame within prophetic moral intelligence is complex and consists of three levels.

Māwardī explains in his classic work on ethics and government, *Adab al-dīn wa al-dunyā*,[132] that three levels of shame can be found within a person. The first is shame before Allah. This is supported by a narration in which the Prophet ﷺ encouraged his Companions to "be shameful before Allah as His Majesty deserves!"[133] The Companions, not quite understanding what he meant, asked for further explanation. The Prophet ﷺ explained, "That you protect your mind and what it contains, that you protect your belly (conscious consumption), that you leave behind overindulgence in the world, and that you remember death."[134] The second level of shame is social shame, or shame before the people, as Māwardī describes it. The third level is an internal shame of one's own self. The first and third levels of shame, from one perspective, can be seen as completely indifferent to the environment and therefore are not necessarily social emotions.

The social value of shame has been explained and defended by Cheshire Calhoun[135] and Jennifer C. Manion[136] in their respective defenses of the positive value of moral shame. Calhoun explains that

---

132 Māwardī, *Adab al-Dīn wa al-Dunyā*, p. 39.

133 Tirmidhī, *Sunan al-Tirmidhī*, vol. 4, p. 218.

134 Ibid.

135 Cheshire, 2004.

136 Manion, 2002.

mature or justified moral shame would only be sensed when one is criticized by people whose opinions one respects and values. Only these people have the power to shame us because we agree to the same moral standard which we ourselves have autonomously chosen. The power we give to others to shame us is simply a reflection of the standards we share with others. Likewise, we can minimize the moral perspective of some people to the point where we aren't affected at all by their criticism; this is considered a sign of moral maturity. I caution Muslims against taking this perspective on shame and morality in general because, in reality, the moral code is not arbitrarily chosen, rather, it is given to us by Allah and exemplified by the Prophet ﷺ. Autonomy simply lies in our choice to follow or not; you really don't have a choice regarding what the moral standards are. However, Calhoun's breakdown of mature moral standards plays a critical role within Islamic moral education in that we are encouraged to develop a thick skin for unwarranted critique.

The third level of shame from the Islamic position involves a completely personalized shame. Moral education will create what is called in the Qur'ānic terminology *al-nafs al-lawwāmah,* or a self-criticizing soul. Regarding the various stages of spiritual maturity, the Qur'ān teaches that there are three stages of development. The lowest level is *al-nafs al-ammārah*, or the commanding self, which perpetually desires other than what Allah has deemed good for the soul. The middle level is *al-nafs al-lawwāmah*, which is mentioned above. The highest level is *al-nafs al-mutma'innah*, which is a soul that is in perfect harmony with the mandates of Allah. The Muslim who has been morally educated and whose moral compass has been calibrated will develop this type of *nafs and* will feel ashamed of any transgressions, even when completely alone. This feeling is not dependent on the views of others because they operate as what Calhoun and others call a "lone moral pioneer."

The *moral pioneer* archetype was introduced as a solution to the aforementioned problem regarding shame's seemingly natural dependence upon others for its functionality. The moral pioneer is a person who has reached a level of morality that surpasses the morality of his society. The conundrum that he finds himself in is that if he treats his people according to their level of morality he would, ideally speaking, feel a sense of shame within himself because he is not upholding his own standard of justice. Nonetheless, he would be free from any blame from the external environment. On the other hand, were he to deal with the people according to his enlightened understanding of morality, he would be at peace with himself for upholding his ideals, but he would be morally critiqued by the broader community. What is the solution?

If we look at the prophets of Allah, we see that the movements they inspired catalyzed moral revolutions within their respective societies. The objective of their divinely inspired missions was to recalibrate the collective moral compass. When approached by his uncle who pleaded with him to refrain from disrupting the social norms and peace of the city, Prophet Muḥammad ﷺ simply replied that he was not able to stop. Muḥammad ﷺ was a moral pioneer. He was the lone custodian of a new standard of appropriateness, a standard of morality that far exceeded the existing standards of his society. Many saw him as the epitome of evil, corrupting the youth of his time. That said, we see that he nonetheless dealt with people according to the new standard which he was given. His ultimate shame was a shame before Allah first, and then before himself. It was not based on people's opinion of him, for the most part. On the contrary, shame before the people was what he tolerated in order to fulfill the command of Allah. I say "for the most part" because a very interesting account, which is related to us through various narrators, tells us not about the sensitivity of the Prophet ﷺ himself, but rather his reaction to being in the presence of someone who also had a very intense sense of shame.

ʿĀ'isha, the wife of the Prophet ﷺ tells us, "The Prophet was once in my house lying down, resting with his thighs or shins exposed. While he was in that position, Abū Bakr came to the door and asked permission to enter. The Prophet, still lying in the same position, granted him permission and they began to converse. A short while later, ʿUmar ibn al-Khattāb arrived at the door and also sought permission to enter. He, too, was given permission and the Prophet ﷺ did not change his position as they began to converse. Finally, ʿUthmān sought permission to enter, whereupon the Prophet ﷺ immediately sat up, straightened out his clothes, and then allowed ʿUthmān to enter and join in the conversation. After they all left, ʿĀ'isha asked the Prophet ﷺ why he didn't fix his clothes and change his position when the other Companions entered but did so when ʿUthmān entered. The Prophet ﷺ replied, "Should I not be shy before a person before whom even the angels are shy?"[137]

This narration brings us to the second level of shame—social shame. The collective ethos and the social disapprobation within the Muslim community can, for some, feel suffocating. Like my friend who turns off the lane departure notification feature on his car because of how intrusive it can become, some people feel that the moral sensitivity and the strong disapprobation within the Muslim community has little to no positive moral influence. But the intrusive nature of social disapprobation does not diminish its positive consequences. Naturally, shame forces one to question two very important factors: (1) why we feel shame; and (2) who we empower to shame us. For a moment, I would like to look back at the roads we drive on every day because there seems to be a cognitive dissonance between how we view practical morality and how we view practical social constructs. As we stated earlier, the most intrusive shaming mechanism we use on the road is the car horn. When we see or encounter a breach in road etiquette (i.e., a breach of a shared standard of conduct) our first means to address the behavior is the car horn. The horn serves as a strong corrective tool because it brings attention to the misconduct of a driver, whoever they may be, and attempts to alert them of their failure to uphold agreed-upon driving norms.

A single, collective moral identity is difficult to achieve within a

137 Muslim, *Ṣaḥīḥ Muslim*, vol. 4, p. 1866.

broad nation-state and has forced religious Muslims to adopt two different standards in public—one Islamic and one non-Islamic. The problem with this approach is that shame reflects our personal identity, our ideal moral self, and our identity should remain constant. The liberal worldview devalues shame and celebrates the individual. In other words, protecting and preserving each driver's choice to drive upon the road as they see fit is the ultimate good. Shame is seen as stunting growth and as a tool of the past to control the masses and dull individual potential. Today, you must be your own judge, jury, and it seems even executioner if need be. The problem that ensues when shame is devalued and demonized is that collective identity and trust are completely lost. This was predicted by the Prophet ﷺ, when he said, "If you have no shame, do whatever you like."[138]

The truth in this narration is the reason why the very concept of moral shame is attacked so fervently. The enlightened revisionist realizes all too well the moral power of shame. This is why they feel they must free humanity from the leash preventing them from exploring their true potential.

If we allow moral sensitivity to revolve solely around identity and give the power to shame only to those with whom we share common ideals, then I foresee only further division of the community. This division is seen in the development of religious "safe spaces," where people can come as they are and feel safe from the annoying, simplistic rants of people who hold the entirety of the *ummah* to a single moral identity. These places are designed to serve those who feel their identity is too nuanced for the general community and those who feel they aren't understood by the general community. But these safe spaces will eventually reach an interesting crossroads where they too will form a common identity between members and they too will, intentionally or unintentionally, agree upon tolerable and intolerable actions, which naturally results in moral identity-related shame—the very thing

138 Imam Mālik, *al-Muwaṭṭā'*, vol. 2, p. 220.

from which they themselves were fleeing. The individual members of these safe spaces will begin to look at themselves as an extension of the group and they too will have shame before other members with whom they share a common identity. By now it should be clear that we cannot remove shame without removing identity.

The difficulty that Muslims in Western countries, and perhaps many predominantly Muslim countries face, is the dual standard of shame that they must learn to navigate, and the constant shifting between two different moral identities. Moral immaturity, or a lack of moral education, allows a person to easily fall victim to unjustified and unwarranted shame. Moral education within our communities should focus on re-centering our values and teach community members what types of criticism to give weight to and how to maintain the moral ideal without completely pushing people away. But most importantly, it should also strive to maintain a collective ideal of morality because this ideal formulates our collective moral identity. And we should differentiate between those who are simply failing to meet the ideal because of human error from those who are actually purposefully attempting to change that identity. The Islamic tri-level construct of shame is beautifully encapsulated in a saying related by Samarqandī,

> One of our pious predecessors said to his son, "When your passions call you to a major sin, then cast your gaze upon the heavens and feel shame before those in the heavens witnessing you. And if that does not create a feeling of shame within you, then cast your gaze to those around you on this earth and feel shame before those witnessing you on the earth. If you don't feel any shame at these two levels, then consider yourself to be from amongst the beasts."[139]

So how do we create a community that doesn't suffocate people who transgress or slip away from the ideal? I believe that the emotional intelligence framework I have outlined is the means by which we develop this moral ideal in others.

139 Samarqandī, *Tanbīh al-Ghāfilīn* p. 47.

IV
Radical Change: How EQ Leads to Real Transformation

As I gathered the information needed to write this book, I became increasingly interested in the relationship between information reception and behavioral modification. At what point does knowing a body of knowledge or set of facts lead to a change in action or behavior, and what are the factors that stop people from modifying their actions to be in line with the information they have acquired? As we have stated many times throughout this book, the role of Prophethood was to convey the message of Allah to humanity and to inspire change within the hearts of those who received the message. Our reliance and belief in *taqdīr* should never prevent us from action and striving to reach our goals. It should not stop us from identifying and studying the barriers to receptivity and the barriers that prevent acquired knowledge from being translated into action. The prophets of Allah used their emotional understanding and intelligence to remove any barriers between their addressees and the message of Allah. They understood that people are often unwilling to accept change, especially *Radical Change*, which by its very nature brings a person to question their own identity, so they had to master the cognitive and emotional factors involved in identity development.

The Qur'ānic narration of the Prophet Yūsuf[140] attempting to call his cellmates to believe in the oneness of Allah demonstrates, on multiple levels, his understanding of human nature and the cognitive and emotional barriers that can prevent a person from being receptive to one's message. First, we see that he waited until they were in need of him. After observing his piety and righteousness, they came to him asking if he could interpret their dreams. Their state of dependency becomes a key factor in influencing how they will perceive any information he gives them because they are already in a state of receptiveness. Thereafter, before he began to explain to them the true message he wished for them to accept, he removed any other barriers by explaining that he would not take a long time. He said to them, "I will tell you the interpretation of your dreams before food is served." He prefaced his message with an assurance that he would not be long-winded, thereby encouraging them to pay close attention. This is an example of his emotional understanding. Interestingly, immediately after giving them this assurance, he says, "This is what my Lord has taught me," suggesting that the revelation given to the prophets has an essential element of emotional understanding.

The Prophet ﷺ, on many occasions, sought refuge with Allah from knowledge that lacked benefit. We are warned by the Prophet ﷺ in countless narrations about the potential danger of learning sacred knowledge without allowing that knowledge to effect change within us. True knowledge is that which fills one's heart and is evident on one's limbs. The Companions of the Prophet ﷺ understood this point well. We find, for example, the story of ʿUmar ibn al-Khaṭṭāb spending over eight years learning the second chapter of the Qur'ān because he would not memorize another verse until he had first put into practice the previous verse. The utility of Prophetic knowledge is that it should

140 Q 12:37.

become the catalyst to reform the life of the one who possesses it. Knowledge without action is ignorance. Khaṭīb al-Baghdādī begins his book, *ʿIqtiḍa al-ʿIlm al-ʿAmal* (*Knowledge Necessitates Action*), explaining the ultimate objective behind seeking prophetic knowledge and its relation to action and reform. He writes;

> I begin by advising you, O seeker of knowledge, to purify your intentions for seeking knowledge. I then advise you to force yourself to act upon that which your knowledge necessitates, because knowledge without action is a tree without fruit.[141]

A few paragraphs later, he explicitly highlights the utility of knowledge. "Knowledge is only sought for actions, just as actions are only done for divine safety. When knowledge doesn't produce actions, then this very knowledge is actually a burden upon the scholar." He supports his entire argument about the intrinsic, inseparable relationship between knowledge and action with a narration in which the Prophet ﷺ said,

> The feet of the children of Adam will not move from their spot on the day of resurrection until they are questioned about four things: how they spent the life they were blessed with; how they acted upon the knowledge they possessed; how they spent the wealth they collected; and lastly, how they used the body they were given.[142]

The scholars of religion learn so that they can act according to the mandates of their knowledge, and they teach to inspire similar praiseworthy actions in others. The problem that teachers face is that learning does not always translate into action, merely transferring information from one mind to the next seldom yields the intended transformation.

The purpose of this section is to present a model for passing on knowledge that inspires "deep change." I use the phrase "deep change" throughout this section because change can happen on many levels,

141 Baghdādī, *Iqtiḍā' al-ʿIlm al-ʿAmal*, p. 14.

142 Tirmidhī, *Sunan al-Tirmidhī*, vol. 4, p. 612.

some of which are more significant than others. By its very nature, the commencement of revelation upon a prophet indicated that deep societal change was needed. What the prophets of Allah brought to humanity sought to cause deep change and reform within the hearts of mankind. But, as we explained before, there are often barriers that obstruct receptivity to the message in the first place or there are barriers that prevent the message from producing the sought-after change. So, what we wish to present here is a method that uses the key elements of emotional intelligence strategically to remove cognitive and emotional barriers to *Radical Change.* By studying this method, we can develop educational programs and community networks that promote positive transformation and development. Again, it's important to stress that this information will have the most utility within our own households. Parents are the first source of education for every child, so they, too, must deeply understand the factors that encourage change and factors that prevent receptivity to change.

Some academics who specialize in how behavioral changes happen within us believe that we have been over-simplifying the most important aspects of education that inspire change. J. P. Walsh says that "We know very little about the social and emotional bases of change and how they relate to each other."[143] Change is a fundamental and constant aspect of life which happens at every instant. For centuries, we have based our pedagogical thought on assumptions about societal and individual change, yet we know so little about ourselves in reality. Hence the pressing need to study the lives and methods of those people who have inspired, and continue to inspire, deep change across nations and generations. Undoubtedly, I am referring to the prophets of Allah. And of the prophets, the one about whom we have the most information is our beloved Prophet Muḥammad ﷺ.

So, what are the underpinnings of societal and individual change? We could begin by unlocking the secrets behind the massive societal

143 Walsh, 1995.

change caused by the Prophet ﷺ within his short 23-year mission. Perhaps if we understood them, we would be more effective teachers, role models, parents, and spouses.

RADICAL CHANGE, SINGLE-LOOP, AND DOUBLE-LOOP EDUCATION

Radical Change has been defined by Quy Nguyen Huy as a "change in the basic philosophy of one person or a shared identity of members of an organization."[144] *Radical Change* is so difficult because it requires that a person start to question a personal or shared identity. Radical change of core beliefs and values often starts with exposing and challenging deep-rooted assumptions. This process is referred to as *double-loop learning.* Double-loop education builds within the mind of the addressee a framework for the change to rest upon. Without developing this framework, the person will not see the need to consider changing, let alone actually implement the change. This process of expose-and-challenge is extremely delicate, and one which many people are not open to because it ultimately deconstructs how they see not only themselves, but also their immediate family and surroundings.

Real change requires a restructuring of understanding. All of the prophets were considered radicals in their times, and they were challenged and resisted because of the deep implications of the message they were sent to convey. In contrast to *double-loop education* is *single-loop education,* which builds upon previously formed assumptions. Single-loop learning occurs when an error is corrected by changing one's behavior, whereas double-loop learning requires changing an underlying assumption, which stimulates a change in behavior and is accompanied by strong emotions. This explains the fervor and drive that normally accompany religious conversion. Single-loop learning will only lead to action and mobilization when the recipients of

144 Huy, 1995.

that information have already constructed the correct framework within which to understand that information. When a person firmly believes in the reward of the hereafter and the Day of Resurrection, for example, simply learning about the reward of a given action will immediately translate into action. This is because the framework that allows that bit of new information to make sense is already in place. On the other hand, if a person lacks strong belief in those things, the newly acquired information may not translate into action because a framework for that bit of information doesn't exist. The framework that results from sound double-loop learning is referred to as a *sense-giving* framework. This is because one is receptive to new information only when a framework exists to make sense of it and give meaning to it. When the framework is established, action and mobilization are immediate. While not the prophetic pedagogical method for inspiring radical change, single-loop learning is used for building good habits and actions after the framework has been established through double-loop learning.

Another way of understanding single—and double-loop learning is to look at how the prophetic mission was divided between Makkah and Madīnah, and the gradation of the *sharīʿah*. Makkah is the place where the foundations of belief were established and the framework of the days of ignorance was uprooted, whereas Madīnah is the place where many of the rulings of Islam were revealed and adopted by Muslims. In terms of our discussion, it would mean that Makkah was the place where a concentrated form of double-loop education occurred and a framework for subsequent single-loop education was built. In Madīnah, when the final revelation regarding the prohibition of wine was revealed, the Muslim community was ready and eager to modify their behavior in ways that would please Allah and His Messenger. But it is essential to note that if the Companions had not received a thorough double-loop education that established the correct framework, they would not have been ready to act when called to do so. This was addressed by the wife of the Prophet, ʿĀ'isha, who said,

> The first revelations of the Qur'ān to be revealed were the chapters from the end of the Qur'ān in which Heaven and Hell were mentioned. Then when people flocked to faith, the verses of permissibility and impermissibility were revealed. If the first thing to be revealed was, "Do not consume wine," then the people would have said, "We will never give up wine!" If the verses regarding the prohibition of fornication had been revealed first, the people would have responded by saying, "We will never give up fornication!"[145]

This narration from ʿĀ'isha specifically addresses a common theme that is found abundantly throughout the Qur'ānic and the prophetic model for moral education. Slow gradation (*tadrīj*) is an essential cornerstone of deep change. It is a process of continual double-loop and single-loop learning. Commenting on this form of single- and double-loop gradation, Ibn Ḥajr al-ʿAsqalānī writes, "She (ʿĀ'isha) is referring to the divine wisdom regarding the gradation within revelation, that the first revelations focused exclusively on calling humanity to the Oneness of Allah, the glad tidings of Paradise for the believers, and the warning of Hellfire for those who disbelieved and disobeyed Allah. Once people's hearts had become content and stable in their belief, the rulings were revealed."[146]

We see another example of this gradual method of education by the Prophet ﷺ when he sent Muʿādh ibn Jabal to the people of Yemen. Imām Bukhārī narrates, "When the Prophet was sending Muʿādh ibn Jabal to the people of Yemen, he said to him, 'Soon you will encounter the people of the book. So, let the first thing that you call them to be the sole worship of Allah. When they have completely understood and recognized that, then tell them that Allah has ordained upon them five prayers throughout their days and nights. When they have established the prayer within their lives, then inform them that Allah has prescribed a mandatory charity upon their wealth to be taken

145 Bukhārī, *Ṣaḥīḥ al-Bukhārī*, vol. 6, p. 185.

146 Ibn Ḥajr, *Fatḥ al-Bārī*, vol. 9, p. 40.

from the wealthy and distributed among the poor. When they agree to that, then take the amount that must be taken, but be careful not to touch their most valued wealth.'"[147]

In order to further grasp both the imperative and complementary nature of both types of learning, focus on what would result if a person was only provided with only one of the two types. Single-loop learning is all about what to do and what not to do. It focuses on immediate behavioral reform and doesn't care about why a particular action should be done. Don't steal, don't lie, don't backbite, don't look at the impermissible, wake up for prayers, do *dhikr* of Allah, avoid wasting time and the list goes on and on. The goal is inner and outer alignment with the do's and don'ts. In other words, our goal is to develop a heart that is ready to know what its Lord wants from it, and ready to live accordingly.

Frameworks for change are continuously established or reinforced in order to facilitate the receptivity of single-loop learning. Without single-loop education, true progress is never made. People need action to reinforce the newly established framework. After double-loop instruction, people have an established framework ready for receiving some commands and prohibition, but if there is an absence of single-loop education they would have failed to receive the action items needed. One can see that if this type of Islamic education persisted without any gradation of single-loop education along with it, a person would never truly reach the point of Radical Change. In fact, I believe that, on the contrary, they would begin to see *themselves* as the criterion of progression. What I mean by this is that knowing the rulings and commands of Allah forces us to constantly strive to reach higher and to realize our deficiencies before Allah, whereas ignorance of the commandments after having established the correct framework can result in one seeing themselves as the ultimate example.

Let me give a more practical example. Let us imagine a person who

147 Bukhārī, *Saḥīḥ al-Bukhārī*, vol. 2, p. 119.

has sat in many lectures regarding the importance of being connected with Allah and always remembering Allah. They truly understand how harmful attachment to anything other than Allah is and they recognize the benefits of having the love of Allah within their heart. Their double-loop education was thus successful. This person, however, was not taught the actions needed to realize a connection with Allah. The person was not taught about the importance of performing the five prayers on time, nor about the verbal statements of remembrance which the Prophet ﷺ regularly engaged in. As a result, this person may feel that they are deeply connected to Allah while at the same time they attach little to no importance to the actions that are the primary means for connecting to Allah.

By now it should be clearer why the Muslims, who believed in the Prophet ﷺ in Makkah, were capable of sacrificing so much. If we look at the story of Bilāl al-Ḥabashī and the torture he endured for the sake of his religion, we can vividly see two aspects mentioned above regarding Radical Change. First, Radical Change is very difficult because of its broader implications for the society and communities that the individuals live in. Secondly, the basis of Radical Change is a process of deep, high-level double-loop learning. While experiencing the sweltering heat of the Arabian sand on his back and a large boulder on his chest, Bilāl simply said, "*He is One! He is One*!" This statement was an expression of the newly established framework that had become embedded in his heart. Although the questioning and challenging of assumptions may come from an external source, the double-loop element of Radical Change, in reality, involves a process of self-discovery. This was exactly the situation with the magicians in the time of Musā. This story, which is repeated many times in the Qur'ān, is about a group of master magicians who were eager to expose and defeat the "magic" of Musā. Hell-bent on humiliating Musā in front of Pharaoh and thousands of spectators, they ultimately end up coming to a deep and profound realization about themselves. This was the moment of *Radical Change* where all of their previously held assumptions were shattered. The *muʿjizāt* or miracles of the prophets of Allah were by themselves powerful inciters of change. The emotional and cognitive barriers to change were instantaneously shattered in light of these miracles. After converting to the religion of Musā, Pharaoh's death threats were completely ineffective because the magicians' understanding of death had changed. The threat of death now translated into the promise of eternal bliss.

The model for *Radical Change* presented by Huy places receptivity at the forefront of all learning and change. Learning and change are inseparably connected because traditional definitions of learning include behavior modification. It has been defined as "a process of acquiring knowledge through experience which leads to a change in behavior."[148] This definition is congruent with the Qur'ānic and prophetic objectives of education and learning. The learning process begins, first and foremost, with receptivity, which simply means that a person allows the message that is being communicated to them to reach their heart and mind. The process of Radical Change ends with two stages: action and maintenance.[149] The Qur'ānic story about the creation of Adam speaks to the innate teachability of human beings. Teachability is a natural aspect of our human disposition. If it is true that we are always increasing in knowledge, this would also necessitate that we are always changing as well. True learning necessitates a change. A problem that we face is that as we grow older and increasingly more and more knowledgeable about the world around us, our receptivity to new information and change decreases. It is important to note that the majority of the people who responded positively to the call of the Prophet ﷺ in the early days of Islam were all relatively young. This is because, as Huy points out, over time we develop barriers or filters that limit the amount of information that we are receptive to. Those barriers to receptivity are primarily of two types—cognitive and

148 Huitt & Hummel, 2006.

149 The process of individual change that has been presented by some specialists consists of five stages: precontemplation, contemplation, preparation, action, and maintenance.

emotional. Before we can begin the process of learning or teaching, which will consequently lead to a change, removal of all cognitive and emotional barriers and filters is necessary.

Developing a sharp emotional intelligence and moral intelligence provides a person with the tools necessary for their message to reach its intended audience. While my intent is to focus primarily on a proactive approach to removing emotional and cognitive barriers, it is important to note that, in the Qur'ān, Allah makes multiple references to a category of people whose actions have blocked their ability to receive the message. These verses come as a type of consolation to the Prophet, primarily, who was deeply grieved by his inability to break through the barriers of some of the individuals he wished to guide.

THE EMOTIONAL FILTERS UP CLOSE

Breaking through the emotional filters requires a deep understanding of the background and current state of the addressee. The more you know about the one you are addressing, the better prepared you will be to avoid the emotional roadblocks that may trigger non-receptivity. Huy is of the opinion that there are three specific conditions that must be met in order to pass successfully through emotional and cognitive filters. The first is that the proposed changes should be compatible with the core values of the addressee. The larger the discrepancy between the two, the more intense the negative emotional response will be. The second condition is that the proposed change must guard the personal welfare of the addressee. These two conditions relate to the content of the proposed change. ʿAdī ibn Ḥātim narrates a detailed account regarding his conversion to Islam which shows that the Prophet ﷺ clearly understood the conditions that must be met for a person to remain receptive to a proposed change.

ʿAdī ibn Ḥātim says, "There was not a single Arab man who hated the Messenger of Allah more than myself when I heard about him and his claim to prophethood. At that time, I was a man of nobility and prestige, I was a Christian, and my position allowed me to live off of one-fourth of the spoils of war. So, I had my own religion and I was a king among my people, so what could this man do for me?" Before we continue the story, it is important to understand who ʿAdī ibn Ḥātim was so that we can gain a better understanding of how his socioeconomic position affected his receptivity to the message of Islam. He was the son of one of the most well-known philanthropists of his time, Ḥātim al-Ṭāʾī. He was comfortable, enjoyed an excellent sociopolitical position, and was looked upon as the king of his people. For him, change was a clear and present danger to his personal welfare. The cognitive sense-making aspect of change is further complicated when we take into consideration a person's socioeconomic position. A person who has been relatively successful at making money and is living comfortably already has confidence in the framework within which they exist. For this person, the saying "If it ain't broke, don't fix it" is perhaps the best way to explain why they are so unreceptive, and sometimes hostile, to radical change. Radical change involves a redefining of understanding, and these people simply don't see the need to redefine anything. Conversely, those who are in economic difficulty tend to be more willing to consider a redefinition of concepts and ideas. There is an emotional and cognitive reason for why they are more receptive, and for them redefinition involves a new opportunity for success. As I have mentioned above, receptivity is all about emotional and cognitive *sense-making* or *sense-giving*. They are urged forward by the hope of becoming successful, and cognitively they are receptive because previous frameworks haven't worked.

As a Christian among the Arabs, ʿAdī ibn Ḥātim enjoyed an extended level of prestige and exclusivity, and with the spread of Islam, this prestige would be lost. Despite the threat to his personal affairs that Islam seemed to pose to him, the Prophet ﷺ was nonetheless very hopeful that ʿAdī would accept Islam due to his sharp intelligence. ʿAdi continues to explain, "When I heard of the Messenger of Allah, I loathed him. I said one day to my slave boy who used to graze my camels, 'Prepare for me obedient, fat camels and keep them close by me. If and when you hear of Muḥammad's army reaching this area, let me know.' He did what I asked him to do. Early one day, he came and said: 'O ʿĀdī! Whatever you planned to do if and when the horsemen of Muḥammad reached you, do it now! I have seen the flags and asked to whom they belong and was told that these are the armies of Muḥammad.' I said, 'Bring my camels to me,' and he did. I traveled with my wife and children, saying to myself that I would join the people who are on my religion, the Christians of the Levant. However, I left behind my sister. When I arrived in the of the Levant, I lived there. Meanwhile, the horsemen of the Messenger of Allah ﷺ attacked our area and took captives. Among those who were captured was my sister. She was brought to the Messenger of Allah ﷺ from among those from Banī Ṭayy who were captured. She was kept in a shed made of trees outside the gate of the mosque where female captives were kept. Later, the Messenger of Allah ﷺ was told about my fleeing to the Levant. One day, he ﷺ passed by her and she stood up to speak to him (she was known to be an eloquent woman), 'O Messenger of Allah ﷺ! The father has died, the caretaker is absent, and I am an old woman and cannot serve anyone. So, bestow a favor on me, may Allah bestow His favor on you.' He ﷺ asked, 'Who is your caretaker?' She said, "ʿAdī ibn Ḥātim!' He ﷺ said, 'The one who fled from Allah and His Messenger?'

ʿAdī's sister further explains, 'So he went away and left me. Early the next day, he passed by me again and I said to him what I said the day before, and he repeated what he said to me the day before. The next day, he again passed by me at a time when I lost hope that he would accept my plea. A man behind me advised me to talk to him again, and I said, 'O Messenger of Allah! ﷺ The father has died, the caretaker is absent, so bestow a favor on me, may Allah bestow His favor on you.' Accepting her request, he replied, 'I will do that, but do not leave in haste until you find a group of your people whom you trust to accompany you to your land; let me know when that happens.'

'I later asked about the man behind me who advised me to talk to the Prophet again, and I was told that it was ʿAli ibn Abī Ṭālib. I stayed in Madīna until a group from (the tribe of) Quḍāʿa came, and I went to the Messenger of Allah ﷺ and said: 'O Messenger of Allah ﷺ, a group from my people has arrived, and they are trustworthy and dependable.' She then said: 'The Messenger of Allah gave me garments as a gift, an animal to ride on, and some money for the trip. I departed with them until I reached the Levant region.'"

Upon accepting her request for freedom, we see that the Prophet ﷺ asked her to stay in Madīnah until she could safely secure the company for the long journey to the Levant. During this time, she was able to freely witness the Islamic society, observe the Muslims in worship, and observe how they interacted with one another. While we can be sure that the Prophet ﷺ was truly concerned about her safety and for that reason did not want her to travel alone, we can also sense a deeper objective behind his request for her to remain because it was during this time that she accepted Islam as a free person living among the Muslim populace. There is no question that the Prophet ﷺ knew that she was a noblewoman and clearly educated and intelligent. The eloquence with which she spoke hints at that. This was a method used very often by the Prophet ﷺ when attempting to guide intelligent people. He would simply encourage them to be in the presence of people who were living Islam and worshipping Allah, for this was, more often than not, the most effective influence for people of reflection.

Continuing his narration, ʿAdī ibn Ḥātim explains, "By Allah, I was sitting with my family when I saw a female rider headed towards me. I said: 'Please be the daughter of Ḥātim,' and it turned out to be her. When she reached us, she started admonishing me, 'The one who cut blood relations, the unjust! You saved your wife and children and left behind the last among the offspring of your father, your own honor!' I said, 'My sister you are speaking nothing except truth. By Allah, I have no excuse, I am guilty of everything you said.' She dismounted from her animal and settled down with us. One day I said to her, 'My sister,' knowing in my heart that she was a wise woman, 'What do you think about this man (the Prophet Muḥammad ﷺ)?' She said (as she was concealing her Islam), 'I think you should go quickly to meet him. If he is a prophet, then those who are foremost to accept him will have a special status. If he is a king, you will never be humiliated while Yemen is mighty, especially since you are who you are (in status and social standing).' I said: 'By Allah, this is sound advice.'"

Notice how she focused on his sociopolitical status. This is the first thing she built her argument around, saying, "If he is a prophet then those who are foremost to accept him will have a special status," which, for ʿAdi, translates into him having an even higher social status than he already enjoys. As we have already pointed out, in order for him to be receptive to the message in the first place, he has to be sure that the proposed change will not negatively affect his personal welfare. Even her second point focused on his social status when she said, "If he is a king, you will never be humiliated while Yemen is mighty, especially since *you are who you are*." She comforted him by reassuring him that, due to his status, he would be safe, regardless of the truthfulness of the Prophet. By now, for ʿAdī, visiting the Prophet ﷺ is a win-win situation. As we have mentioned, she had already accepted Islam, but she doesn't reveal that to him for fear that he may discredit her advice due to a conflict of loyalties.

> I left (the Levant) heading towards the Messenger of Allah ﷺ in Madīna. I first approached him while he was in the mosque and greeted him. The people started whispering around us saying, "This is ʿAdī!" I went there without a truce or any promise of safety. When I reached him, he took my hand and he said that he hoped that Allah would place my hand in his hand. Then, the Prophet of Allah ﷺ stood up and took me to his house.

The first thing that ʿAdi remembers about his first meeting with the Prophet ﷺ is the physical contact that the Prophet ﷺ initiated. In earlier chapters, we spoke about the power of touch and how a sense of immediacy between two people can be felt by one's eagerness to be in physical contact with another person. Reaching out to shake the hand of ʿAdī, the Prophet ﷺ is expressing to him that, although this was their first time meeting, that he was eager to be close to ʿAdī and that he was comfortable with him.

The Prophet ﷺ understood that all cognitive and emotional barriers had to be removed in order for ʿAdī to properly receive the message of Islam, and the first step toward that was a gentle touch. The Prophet ﷺ further solidifies within the mind of ʿAdī that he has a special place in his heart by telling him that he had hoped Allah would place ʿAdī's hand in his hand. One can only imagine how flattered ʿAdī must have felt at this, as others looked on and listened. This was the first step to removing the emotional barriers that could have stopped the message. ʿAdī continues, "While he was taking me there, a weak old woman met him, asked him to talk to her, and he ﷺ stood with her for a long time while she was explaining her need to him. I said to myself, 'I swear by Allah, this is not (the behavior of) a king.'"

This is perhaps one of the strongest passages regarding the empathy and the selflessness that the Prophet ﷺ was taught by his Lord. We must keep in mind that when ʿAdī left his sister's company, they agreed that Muḥammad ﷺ could either be a prophet or a king. As he spends time with the Prophet ﷺ, he is attempting to deduce from the Prophet's ﷺ actions which of the two best suits him. In this part of the narrative, we are told that an elderly, weak woman, with obviously little to no political influence or power, stops the Prophet as he intends to speak to a man of high nobility. ʿAdī is a king himself so he knows what he is looking for. He knows that a king would not stand humbly, patient and attentive for someone who, outwardly, has no power or influence. So as the Prophet ﷺ stood before this woman as if she was the Emperor of Rome, ʿAdī recognizes that this man could only be a Prophet of Allah. In other words, he was able to deduce from the level of importance that Muḥammad ﷺ attributed to the weakest of his community that he was truly a man of Allah. In this situation we see that it was love and empathy that removed yet another potential barrier from the pathway of guidance and acceptance.

ʿAdī continues, "The Messenger of Allah ﷺ then took me to his house, picked a cushion made of wool and stuffed with leaves, and gave it to me saying: 'Sit on this.' I said: 'Rather, you sit on it.' He ﷺ, said: 'No, you sit on it,' and he sat on the bare floor. I said to myself, 'By Allah, this is not a king.' He ﷺ then said to me: 'O ʿAdī ibn Ḥātim, embrace Islam and you will acquire safety.' I said: 'I am following a religion.' He ﷺ again said: 'O ʿAdī ibn Ḥātim, embrace Islam and you will acquire safety.' I said: 'I am following a religion.' He ﷺ, said: 'I am more knowledgeable about your religion than you are.' I replied: 'You are more knowledgeable about my religion than I am?' He ﷺ said: 'Yes.' Then he ﷺ, said: 'O ʿAdī ibn Ḥātim, are you not a follower of Rakūsīyyah [a Christian sect that mixed Christianity with fire worship]?' I said: 'Yes.' He ﷺ said: '[When you fought alongside your tribe], did you not take a fourth of the war-booty from your people?' I said: 'Yes.' He ﷺ said: 'That is not allowed for you in your religion.' I said: 'By God, it is true what you say.' I knew at that moment that he ﷺ was a sent Prophet who knows what others do not know."

Before discussing this portion of the narration, we should look at the last of the three conditions that must be met in order for the proposed change to pass through all cognitive and emotional barriers. According to Huy, the third condition is having trust in the agent of change. The one to whom the change is proposed must have complete trust in the one presenting the idea. Huy further breaks down this trust into two types. The first type is called cognitive trust and is based on the perception of competence and reliability, and the second type is called affective trust that is based on sensing genuine care and concern from the agent of change. When the Prophet ﷺ brought ʿAdī into his house and insisted that ʿAdī sit on the only available cushion while he himself sat on the bare floor, ʿAdī became increasingly aware that the man he was dealing with had a deep care and concern for all those whom he interacted with. This led him to acknowledge that the Prophet did not act like a king. The next conversation that took place involves the Prophet's explicit invitation to Islam, along with ʿAdī's rebuttal that he already had a religion. The Prophet ﷺ then begins to teach ʿAdī about his own religion and actions that ʿAdī was doing which were not allowed according to ʿAdī's faith. This seems to serve two purposes. First, it displayed to ʿAdī how knowledgeable the Prophet ﷺ was regarding the previously revealed religions. Doing so acknowledges ʿAdī's desire to worship Allah and conveys to him that Islam is the means by which to do so. Had the Prophet ﷺ displayed a lack of knowledge regarding ʿAdī's faith, it could have appeared that the Prophet was unaware of such important matters. The second effect of this conversation is that by pointing out that ʿAdī's actions were not in line with his own religion's teachings, the Prophet forced him to internally question his true commitment to his faith. By this point in the conversation, it seems that ʿAdī was very close to admitting his faith in the Oneness of Allah and the truthfulness of the Prophet. At that moment, something happens which, seemingly, has the potential to completely undo all the progress that the Prophet ﷺ has made. As we mentioned above, ʿAdī's sister understood the importance which ʿAdī placed on maintaining his social status, and she used that to persuade him to go and meet the Prophet ﷺ. Similarly, we have mentioned that Huy has pointed out that the security of personal welfare and well-being is a condition that must be met in order to assure the message is not lost. ʿAdī explains what happened next,

> While I was with the Prophet of Allah ﷺ, a man came to him complaining of poverty, then another man came complaining of lack of safety on the pathways." These two complaints had a deep impact on ʿAdī's ability to make a rational decision. The Prophet ﷺ immediately noticed this and successfully removed the emotional barrier that arose as a result of these two men's complaints. He said, "ʿĀdī, perhaps what prevents you from embracing this religion is what you witness of their poverty. I swear by Allah that, soon,

> wealth will increase for them so much so that there will be no one to take charity. Perhaps what prevents you from embracing it is that their enemies are numerous, and their numbers are lacking. By Allah, soon a woman would leave Qādisiyya while riding her camel, until she visits the Kaʿbah in Makkah without any fear.

After addressing the fears that crept into the mind of ʿAdī, the Prophet ﷺ returned to the issue of social status and political power. ʿAdī said, "I said to myself, 'What about the wicked men of Ṭayy who filled the earth with mischief? Where will they be then?'" Although ʿAdī did not vocalize this concern, the Prophet ﷺ sensed his concern and said, "Maybe what prevents you from embracing it is that you see kingship and might with others. By Allah, you will soon hear that the white palaces of Babylon have been opened for them." ʿAdi concludes this narration saying, "I embraced Islam and noticed happiness on the Prophet's face."[150]

For ʿAdī, his conversion to Islam took some time because he had to experience and witness the sincerity, truthfulness, and empathy that the Prophet ﷺ was blessed with. For those who knew the Prophet ﷺ closely prior to Islam, the conversion was often instantaneous. Regarding the conversion of Abū Bakr, Ibn Isḥāq and others narrate, "He (Abū Bakr) was a close friend of the Prophet ﷺ prior to the commencement of the revelation. He was fully aware of his truthfulness, trustworthiness, pure nature, and that he possessed such an upright character that he was prevented from lying about the creation, so how could he lie about the Creator? For this reason, when the Prophet ﷺ told him that Allah had sent him, he accepted the call immediately."[151]

150 Ibn Kathīr, *al-Sīra al-Nabawiyya*, vol. 4, p. 125.

151 Ibn Kathīr, *al-Bidāya wa al-Nihāya*, vol. 3, p. 27.

Conclusion

Our analysis of the Prophet Muḥammad's ﷺ intellect as a type of emotional and moral intelligence inspired by revelation just begins to scratch the surface of the prophetic model of intelligence. It is imperative that followers of the Abrahamic faiths collectively display to humanity precisely how the intellect is designed to be used. The role and function of the intellect is not merely to subjugate the world and place mankind at the top of the food chain. Rather, the intellect is a humble guide that yearns for the light of God to know itself and to know where it must go and how it must act. Without the development of emotional intelligence, we run the risk of destroying perhaps the most valuable aspect of our lives—our families. The consequences of weakening, or even worse, destroying the institution of family are grave. Mary Eberstadt explains in her book, *How the West Really Lost God,* that in the West and across the world there is a direct correlation between the rise and fall of religious life with the growth and deterioration of family life. Her studies show that as a family grows and becomes closer, members of the family are more likely to see themselves as religious people. They are more likely to go to church and be a part of a religious community. At the beginning of this book, we presented a study that showed that as Americans became more "intelligent," their religious belief decreased. What the study failed to show is how those changes affected family life in America. The reality is that family life in America was deteriorating as people became less religious. The revelation sent down upon Muḥammad ﷺ places five things at the forefront of human existence: life, religion, family, intellect, and wealth. The preservation of these five areas is considered the entire purpose of Islam and, presumably, other Abrahamic faiths. Through our current study, one should see that just as religious identity and the health of the family relationship are directly correlated, so too is the strength of the intellect an indicator of family and religious strength. It is as if the strength and weakness of one of these five areas reveals a potential strength and weakness of the rest.

The collective level of a family's emotional intelligence is a key indicator of the well-being and strength of that family unit. The studies and the work of Dr. Eberstadt mentioned above lead us to conclude that, as prophetic intellect decreases in society, family life begins to deteriorate, thereafter resulting in the crumbling of the institution of religion. The Prophet's ﷺ ability to manage multiple households harmoniously shows the magnitude of his emotional intellect. It is quite reasonable, then, to suggest that as a family grows larger, so too does the need for one's emotional intelligence. Similarly, the level of emotional intelligence needed to maintain meaningful, nurturing relationships on a communal level is far greater than that needed for the one living away from the rest of society. The popular understanding of intelligence is playing a destructive role in family and communal life. The increasing need for daycare and elderly care facilities speaks to the decrease in intelligence, or at least a shift in the meaning of intelligence. Children and the elderly in our communities both demand a significant amount of emotional labor and if one wishes to nurture meaningful interactions with either of these two groups, they must possess a high level of emotional intelligence. As a culture, we have attempted to outsource the emotional burden of caring for these people. But why would we need to do this if we are so much more intelligent than premodern people?

Perhaps as we redefine intelligence, we will, in the process, regain the value of family and religion.

Selected Bibliography

Ḥajar, I. (1996). *Fatḥ al-Bārī.* Cairo: Maktab Taḥqīq Dār al-Ḥaramayn.

Alegre, A. (2012). The relation between the time mothers and children spent together and the children's trait emotional intelligence. *Child Youth Care Forum*, 41, 493–508.

Al-Qayyim. (1998). *Miftāḥ Dār al-Saʿādah.* Cairo: Dār al-Ḥadīth.

al-Qayyim, I. (2017). *Igāthat al-Lahfān.* (M. I. Saʿīd, Ed.) Makkah, Saudi Arabia: Dār ʿĀlam al-Fawā'id.

Bābartī. (2009). *Sharḥ Waṣiyyat Abu Ḥanīfah.* (Ḥ. al-Bakrī, Ed.) Amman, Jordan: Dār al-Fatḥ.

Badri, M. (2013). *Abū Zayd al-Balkhī's Sustenance of the Soul: the Cognitive Behavior Therapy of a Ninth Century Physician.* Herndon, Virginia: The International Institute of Islamic Thought.

Baghdādī. (1977). *Iqtiḍā' al-ʿIlm al-ʿAml.* Beruit: Maktab al-Islāmī.

Bauman. (1993). *Modernity and Ambivalence.* Cambridge: Polity Press.

Bayhaqī. (2003). *Shuʿab al-Īmān* (Vol. 6). Bombay, India: Maktabah al-Rushd.

Bukhārī. (1998). *Al-Adab al-Mufrad.* Riyad: Maktab al-Maʿārif.

Cheshire, C. (2004). An Apology for Moral Shame. *The Journal of Political Philosophy*, 12(2).

Dawūd, A. (2000). *Sunan Abū Dawūd.* (M. M. al-Dīn, Ed.) Beirut: Maktab al-ʿAṣriyyah.

Dhahabī. (2006). *Siyar Aʿlām al-Nubalā'* (Vol. 9). Cairo, Egypt: Dār al-Ḥadīth.

Field, T. (2003). *Touch.* Cambridge: MIT Press.

Gallace, A., & Spence, C. (2008). The Science of Interpersonal Touch; An Overview. *Neuroscience and Biobehavioral Reviews*, 246–259.

Gardner. (2011). *Frames of Mind: The Theory of Multiple Intelligences.* New York: Basic Books.

Ghazālī. (1987). *Miskhāt al-Anwār.* Beirut: ʿĀlam al-Kutub.

Ghazālī. (1989). *The Alchemy of Happiness.* (H. A. Homes, Ed.) Albany, New York: University Mircofilms International.

Ghazālī. (2011). *Iḥyā' ʿUlūm al-Dīn* (Vol. 1). Jeddah, Saudi Arabia: Dār al-Minhāj lil al-Nashar wa al-Tawzīʿ.

Goleman, D. (1997). *Emotional Intelligence.* New York: Bantam Books.

Green, L. (2017, April 1). The trouble with Touch? New Insights and Observations on Touch for Social Work and Social Care. *The British Journal of Social Work*, 47(3), 773–792.

Gregory, B. (2015). *The Unintended Reformation.* Harvard University Press.

Hertenstein, M. J., & Keltner, D. (2006). Touch communicates distinct emotions. *Emotion*, 3(6), 528–533.

Huitt, W., & Hummel, J. (2006). An overview of the behavioral perspective. *Educational Psychology Interactive.*

Huy, Q. N. (1995). Emotional Capability, Emotional Intelligence, and Radical Change. *Academy of Management Review*, 24(2), 235–245.

Karamali, H. (2017). *The Madrasa Curriculum in Context.* Kalam Research & Media.

Kathīr, I. (1988). *Al-Bidāyah wa al-Nihāyah.* Dār Iḥyā' Turāth al-Kutub al-ʿArabiyyah.

Kathīr, I. (1990). *Al-Bidāyah wa al-Nihāyah* (Vol. 10). Beirut: Maktab al-Maʿārif.

Kekes, J. (1993). *The Morality of Pluralism.* Princeton: Princeton University Press.

Kreeft. (1996). *Ecumenical Jihad; Ecumenism and the Culture War.* San Francisco: Ignatius Press.

Kreeft. (2010). *Socratic Logic.* South Bend: St. Augustine's Press.

Kreeft, P. (1999). *A Refutation of Moral Relativism: Interviews with an Absolutist.* San Francisco: Ignatius Press.

Linden, D. (2015). *Touch; The Science of the Hand, Heart, and Mind.* Penguin.

Mājah, I. (2009). *Sunan Ibn Mājah* (Vol. 5). (S. al-Arnaʿūṭ, Ed.) Dār al-Risālah ʿĀlamiyyah.

Māwardī. (2013). *Adab al-Dīn wa al-Dunyā.* Beruit: Dār al-Minhāj.

Maḥbūbī. (n.d.). *Tanqīḥ.* Arambagh: Qadīmī Kutub Khānah.

Makari, G. (2015). *Soul Machine; The invention of the Modern Mind.* New York: W. W. Norton & Company.

Mangera, AR. (2007). *Imām Abū Ḥanīfa's Al-Fiqh al-Akbar Explained.* London: White Thread Press.

Manion, J. C. (2002). The Moral Relevance of Shame. *American Philosophical Quarterly*, 39(1).

Mehrabian, A. (1971). *Silent Messages.* Belmont, California : Wadsworth Publishing.

Muḥāsibī. (1971). *Al-ʿAql wa fahm al-Qur'ān.* (Ḥ. al-Quwwaytalī, Ed.) Damascus: Dār al-Fikr.

Munẓarī. (2007). *Al-Targīb wa al-Tarḥīb.* (I. S. al-Dīn, Ed.) Beruit: Dār al-Kutub al-ʿAlimiyyah.

Muslim. (N/A). *Ṣaḥīḥ Muslim.* Beirut: Dār ʿIḥyā al-Turāth al-ʿArabiyyah.

Qurṭubī. (1964). *Tafsīr Qurṭubī.* (A. al-Bardūnī, Ed.) Cairo: Dār al-Kutub al-Miṣriyyah.

Qutaybah, I. (1990). *Al-Imāmah wa al-Siyāsah* (Vol. 2). (ʿ. Sherī, Ed.) Beirut, Lebanon: Dār al-Aḍwā'.

Rāzī. (1999). *Tafsīr al-Kabīr.* Beirut: Dār Iḥyā Turāth al-ʿArabiyyah.

Samarqandī. (2000). *Tanbīh al-Ghāfilīn.* Damascus: Dār Ibn Kāthīr.

Smith. (2010). *The Disenchantment with Secular Discourse.* Cambridge: Havard University Press.

Suyūtī, J. a.-D. (2004). *Tārīkh al-Khulafā'.* (Ḥ. al-Damardāsh, Ed.) Makkah: Maktab Nezār Muṣṭafā.

Tabrīzī. (1985). *Miskhāt al-Maṣābīḥ.* (Albānī, Ed.) Beirut: Maktab al-Islāmī.

Taftāzānī. (n.d.). *Sharḥ al-Talwīḥ.* Qadīmī Kutub Khānah.

Tanner, C., & Christen, M. (2013, Jan). Moral Intelligence—A Framework for understanding Moral Competences. *Empirically Informed Ethics*, 119–136.

Tarnas. (1991). *The Passion of the Western Mind.* New York: Ballantine Books.

Tirmidhī. (1998). *Sunan al-Tirmidhī.* (B. ʿAwād, Ed.) Beirut: Dār al-Garb al-Islāmī.

Walbridge. (2011). *God and Logic and Islam.* Cambridge: Cambridge University Press.

Walsh, J. (1995, May–June). Managerial and Organizational Cognition. *Organization Science*, 6(3).

Zuhaylī. (2000). *Al-Fiqh al-Islāmī wa Adillatuhu.* Damascus: Dār al-Fikr.